ISBN: 978-0-9890085-2-5

www.lilyannabel.com

Updates From Lily 2012

(Watchin' the Beeb)

Andy Stowe

Introduction

OK, I tried to write something poignant or insightful for the intro here but I'm sorry to advise that it's tricky and I'm tired. No dice. Allow me to say simply: For our grandparents, whom we love dearly but not so much that we want them here every day watching this stuff in person.

Table of Contents

May

Embarrassment first

Posted on May 4, 2012

OK, let's get this out of the way. We call her the 'Bebus'. Derived from 'bebe', which I think is maybe Spanish and which appears in the instruction manuals for many things we own. Anyway, if 'bebe' is the plural, we reasoned 'Bebus' must be the singular. Such is our deep understanding of the Spanish language.

So that's the embarrassing pet name for now. The Bebus. The Beeb. If she's looking strong, Beebtocules (from Hercules). If she had bolts in her neck, Frankenbeeb. You get the idea.

Posted in Uncategorized | 3 Replies

Julia = the binker.

Ruby = the babe, as in "the babe abides"

- Aunt Kristen

To us, she will always also be SARGE

- Grandma A

Full support for references to The Big Lebowski and Sargeant Slaughter. Well played!

- Editor

3

DC in the house

Posted on May 5, 2012

Auntie E.

First, normal:

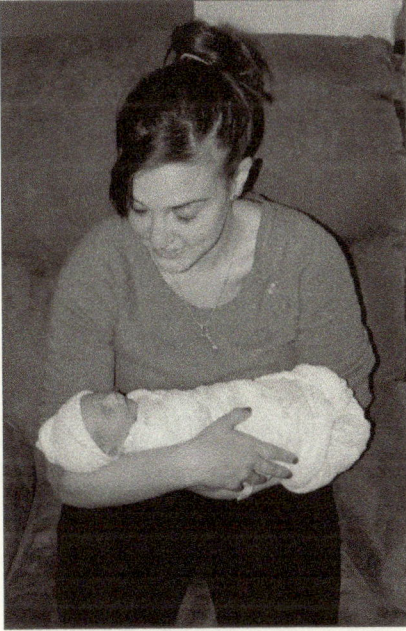

Second: with over-the-top cheeseball grin:

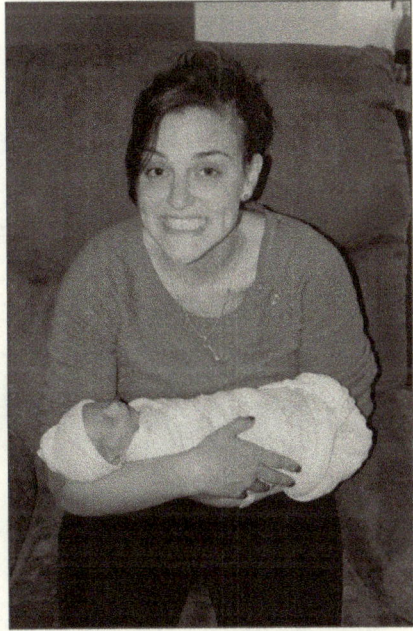

Posted in Meet the bebe

4

Berryville in the house

Posted on May 6, 2012

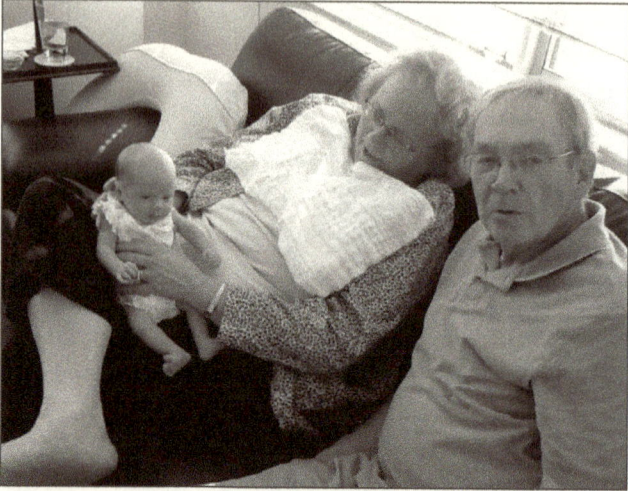

Posted in Meet the bebe

Lily rules

Posted on May 8, 2012

Chillin' on a Sunday morning, listening to Elvis and drinking milk.

Posted in pics | 1 Reply

Love it! Where's mama?

- Aunt Kristen

They had a pool and a pond

Posted on May 9, 2012

Will update soon with shots from our wildly successful trip to Central Park yesterday. We had kids aplenty from the Mike & Kellys, the Kerry & Genines, the Seth & Alis (Luca counts!), and of course Michael C. Big win: nobody pooped their pants without a diaper on.

Posted in Uncategorized

The Colossus of Hell's Kitchen

Posted on May 10, 2012

Little Ms. Lily weighed in at a porky 6 lbs, 14oz on Friday. I'm entering her in the annual Coney Island Hot Dog Eating Contest this year. Not everyone can add 50% to their weight in a month, you know…not even the Summer of Michael was that effective! Our expectation is that she will be roughly 400 lbs by Memorial Day.

Quoth the bebus, "Follow your dreams. You can meet your goals. I'm living proof. Beefcake! BEEFCAKE!!!"

Suck it, Rhodes.

Posted in Uncategorized

Posing

Posted on May 11, 2012

She's been a complete pain in the butt today. Wants to eat every hour or so…no naps to speak of. Standing up an awful lot though. With help, of course.

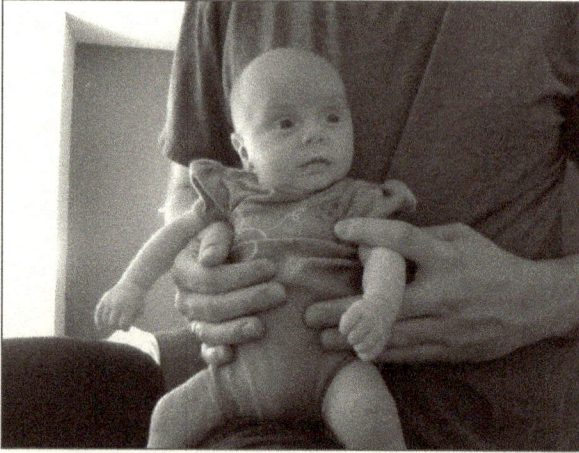

Posted in pics

She outgrew something!

Posted on May 12, 2012

Dude, she outgrew some preemie clothes! I'm running around like Navin Johnson with a new phonebook.

Thankfully, we have gobs of clothes and don't need to replace this in the wardrobe rotation. But this, I fear, is how it begins…

Posted in pics | 1 Reply

Be afraid…

- Aunt Kristen

10

The full body yawn

Posted on May 13, 2012

Lily is a champion yawner.

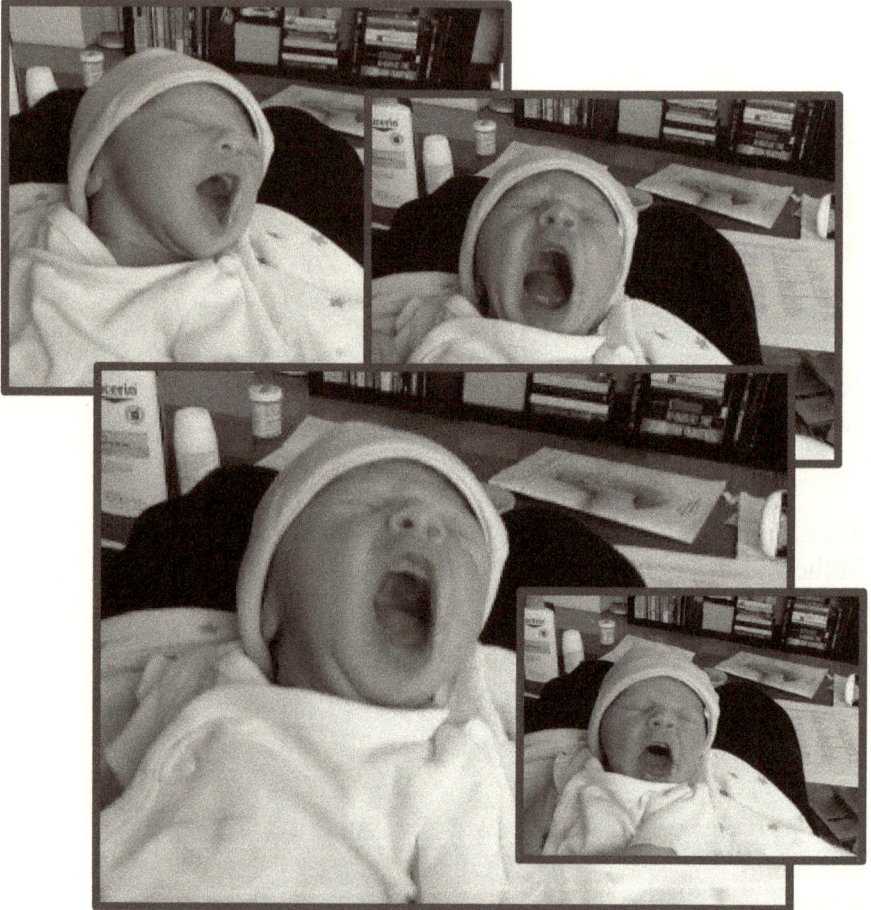

Posted in Uncategorized | 1 Reply

The ol' yawn & drool. Classic move.

- Dad

11

Babies: Not smart yet

Posted on May 15, 2012

You can try to nurse through my harley-davidson t-shirt. But even if you succeeded, you would find only my unpleasant hairy chest and unfunctioning nipples. You would be disappointed, for sure. So quit trying to nurse on me. It makes no sense, dummy.

Posted in Uncategorized

Baby nature vs. the chair

Posted on May 16, 2012

Vibrochair rocks.

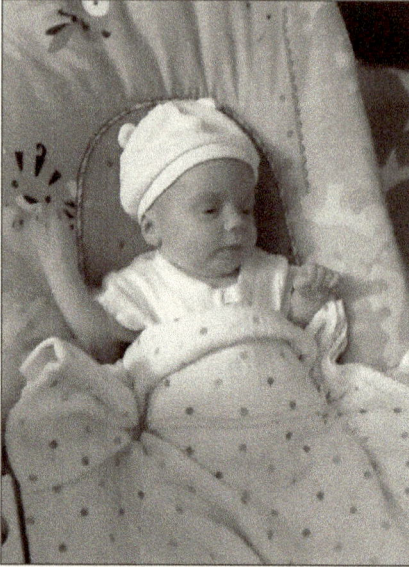

But it was not enough to overcome tiredness, hunger, and the anger bomb inside.

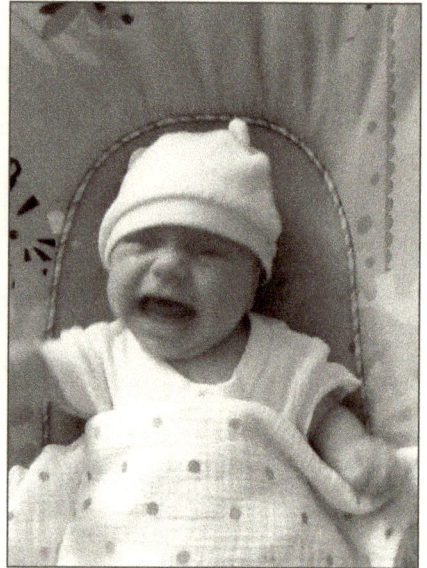

Final score: Baby nature: 1, Vibrochair 0.

It's hilarious when that hat drops over her eyes. But then she gets grumpy about it and it's not hilarious any more.

Posted in Uncategorized

Poop face

Posted on May 17, 2012

She's already toning down her use of the poop face. That's a drag, 'cause it was awesome. She'd purse her lips and then her eyes would start darting back and forth. You knew that was the sign…

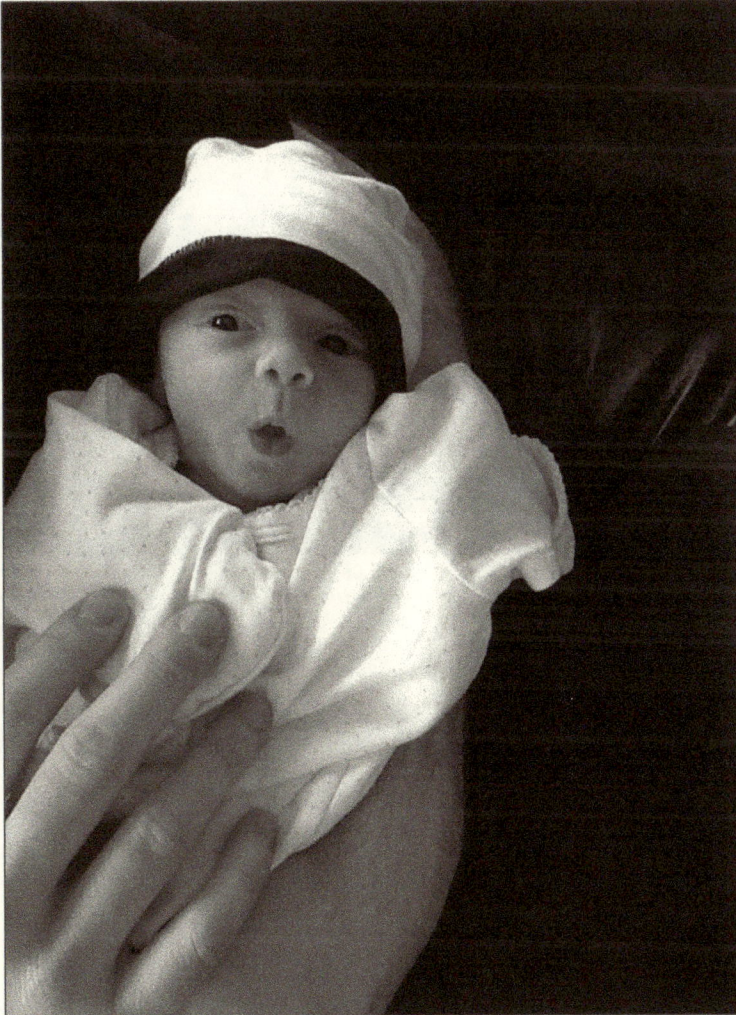

Chicago in the house

Posted on May 18, 2012

Auntie BA of BARF fame displaying impressive bebe-whispering skills.

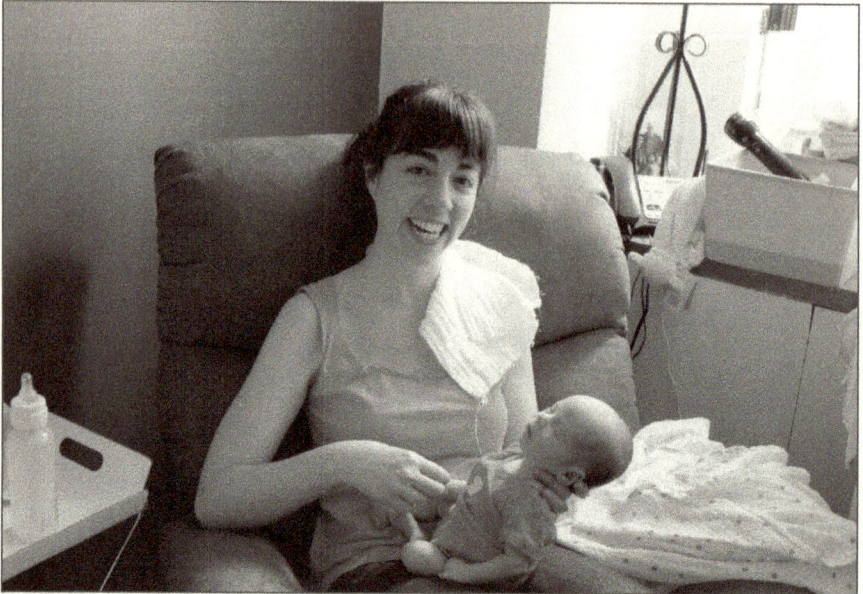

Posted in Meet the bebe

NY in the house

Posted on May 19, 2012

Auntie G.

Posted in Meet the bebe

Successful road trip!

Posted on May 20, 2012

Made it all the way to DC and back! We took the long way and the slow roads (the better to pull over quickly in the event of a meltdown)…but we made it with minimal scathing. Define 'minimal', you say? Well, there was a quasi-panicked stop at the world's most depressing rest area. Lily flipped and screamed so hard that she sweated through her clothes. But we made it, which means we're potentially mobile! Victory is ours!

Posted in Uncategorized

Us in the DC house

Posted on May 21, 2012

Many many thanks to Colin & Patty for having us over! Not only did we get to catch up with good friends (Maria was there too), we were able to glean a little parenthood advice. We need it desperately.

Choice tidbits:
Maria: Children are virtually indestructable. Go ahead. Try it out.*
Patty: Make sure to mix a little tabasco sauce in with their meals to toughen them up.*
Colin: Revenge is a dish that is best served cold. Plan revenge on your kids. Then chill them.*

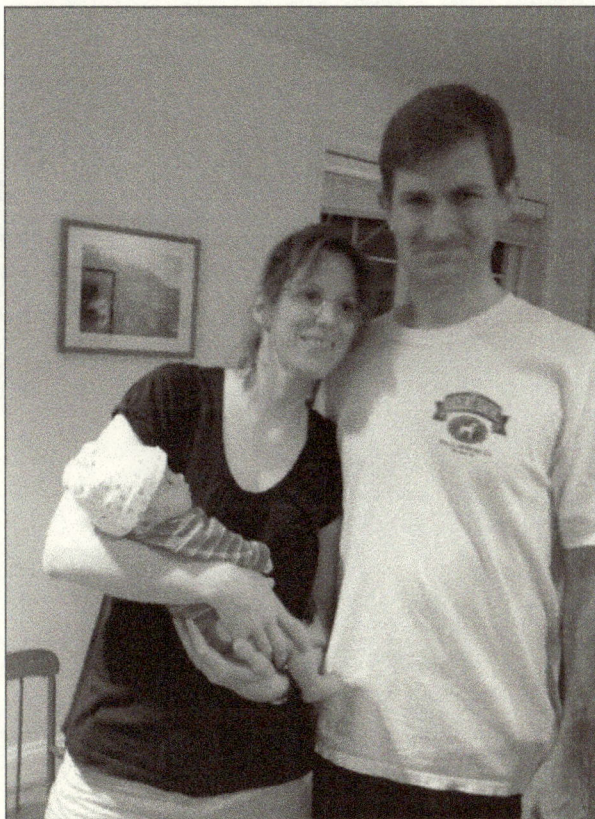

* not an actual quote or suggestion.

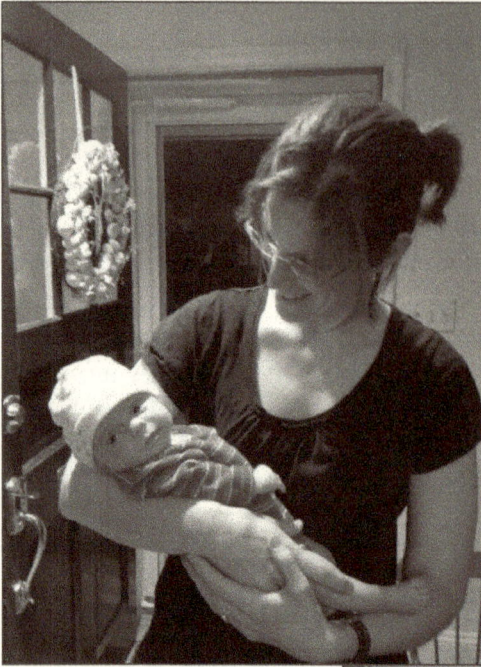

Posted in Meet the bebe

Crazy coordinated

Posted on May 23, 2012

Well, not really. She looked like she was holding the bottle herself…but then I moved her hands and the bottle didn't move at all. Hands unnecessary. She holds it in place…*with her mind.*

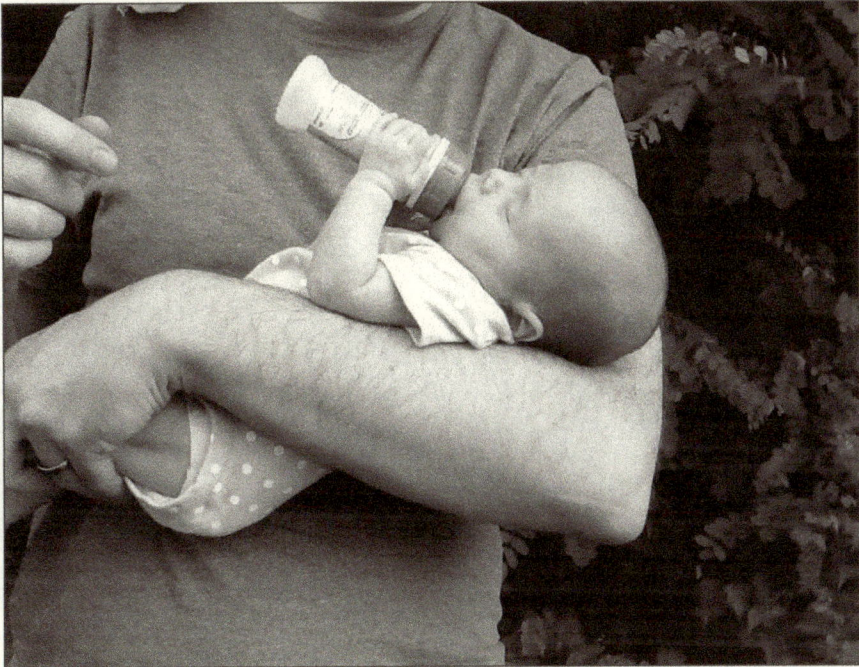

What the hell happened here?

Posted on May 24, 2012

Was she in a fist fight? Did she get into daddy's scotch? Was she the victim of a tear gas attack? We may never know. She's OK now though.

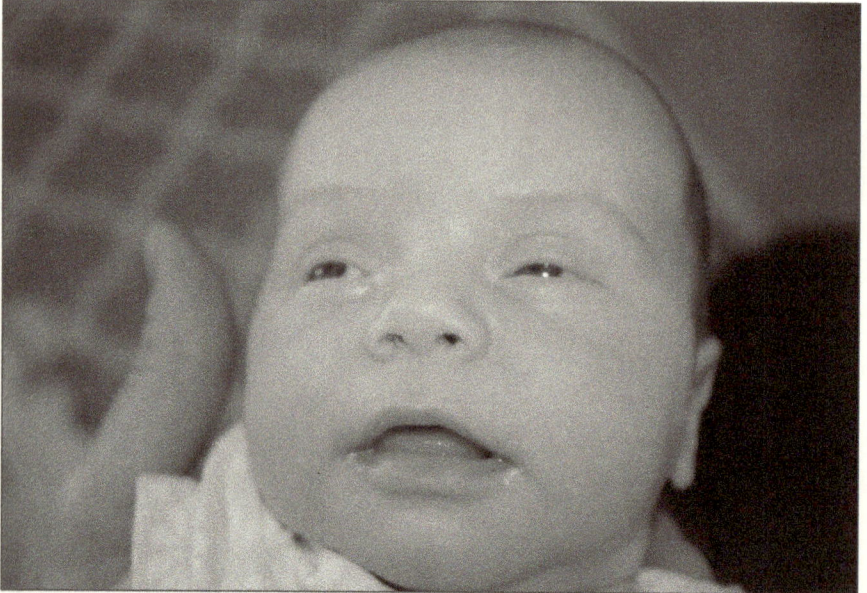

That's cute

Posted on May 25, 2012

Nuff said. Note daddy absent from pic, thus preserving its cuteness.

Posted in pics

Auntie Bex back for more

Posted on May 26, 2012

We're pleased to have Becky back in the house to offer some much-needed support. She was part of our rapid response team this morning after Lily barfed all over the place and then Kathy fell asleep. Her rapid response? Hold the bebe so I could go to work and Mama Kath could finally get a few minutes' sleep. That's damn fine work!

(OK, it was spitting up, not barfing. Nothing scary. And Mama was 'a point' to be clear. But then sleepy.)

Posted in Uncategorized

23

Down goes Frazier!

Posted on May 27, 2012

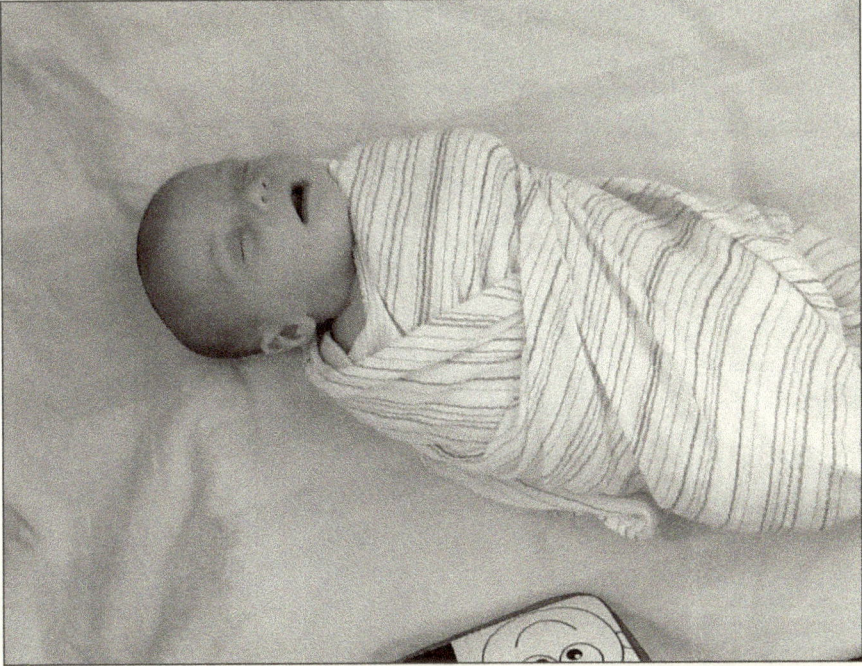

Posted in pics

Our HVAC Rules (guest post!)

Not sure how one baby can be so cute. Also, Kathy and I have realized that she sounds remarkably like the HVAC system and the elevators in the building, which all make adorable cooing noises. I never knew I could love an HVAC system so much.

- Auntie B

Posted in Guest Post!

25

Grandma: Made of Sedatives

Posted on May 30, 2012

Lily tried to bite Grandma's finger off, but was stopped in her tracks by the powerful nerve agents seeping from the hand pores. Yes, hand pores. That's the best I could do.

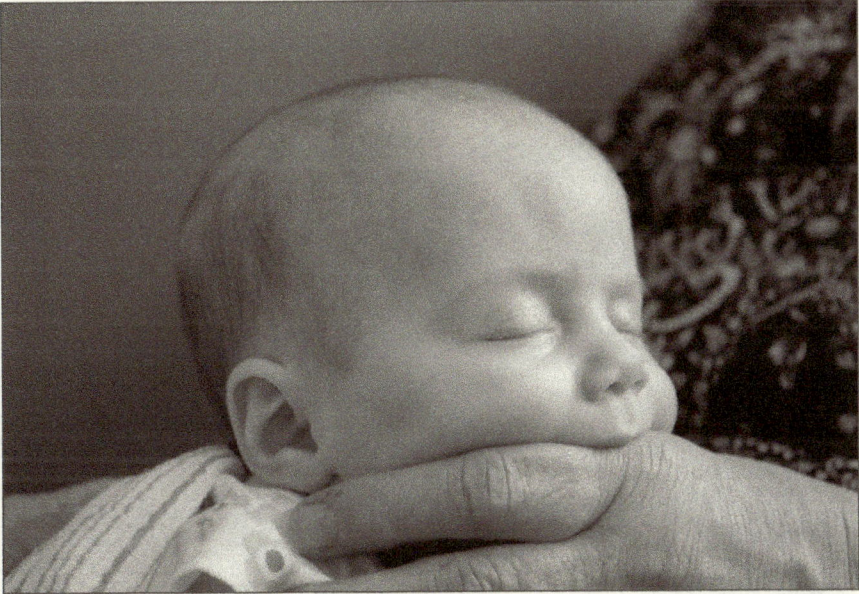

Posted in pics

Party time (Pass the Bebus to the left hand side)

Posted on May 31, 2012

Pulled off a quasi-brilliant surprise birthday party for Mama Stowe on Thursday night. The Bebe? Passed around like Boone's Farm at a high school mixer. And slept like a champ pretty much the whole time. Appears she may be a social animal when the mood's right.

With Jisook:

With Michelle:

Posted in Meet the bebe

June

Estimated 28% Basset Hound

Posted on June 1, 2012

She got the drool genes, not the floppy ears. Victory! Now awaiting a shot at the casting agents for the Smokey & The Bandit remake that is so desperately needed. Playing the role of Fred, of course. My girl Fred. A proud moment.

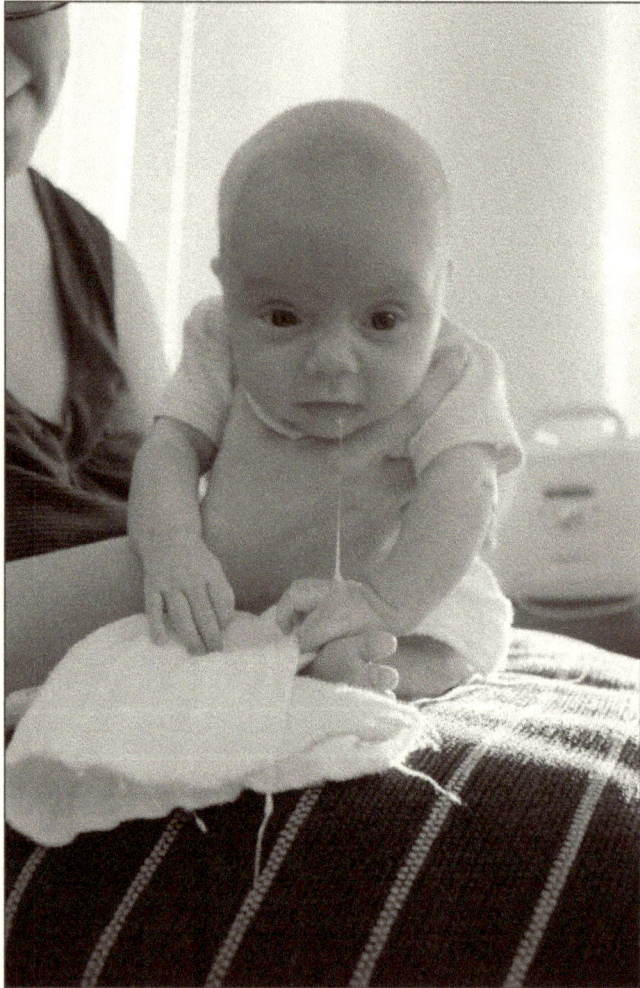

Posted in pics

31

Quick! They went that way!

Posted on June 2, 2012

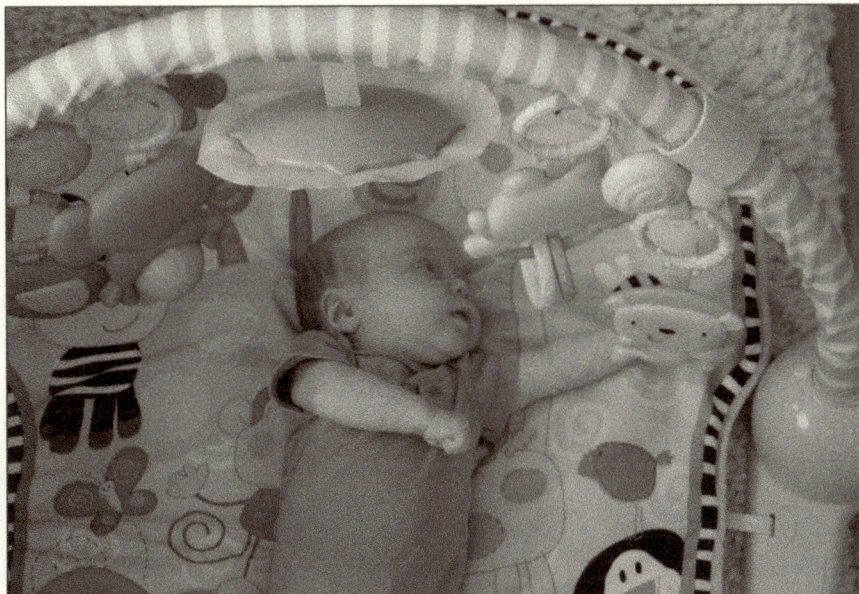

Posted in pics

Sleep when the baby sleeps

Posted on June 3, 2012

Advice heeded! It's been a tough morning, and although this pic wasn't taken today it sort of captures the mood. I got the 2am feeding and the Bebe was WFA (wide awake) until 3:30 when she finally crashed and burned. By then, of course, I was up. The whole family's had their schedule thrown out the window. Oh for the peaceful moments where mom and Bebe sleep peacefully together.

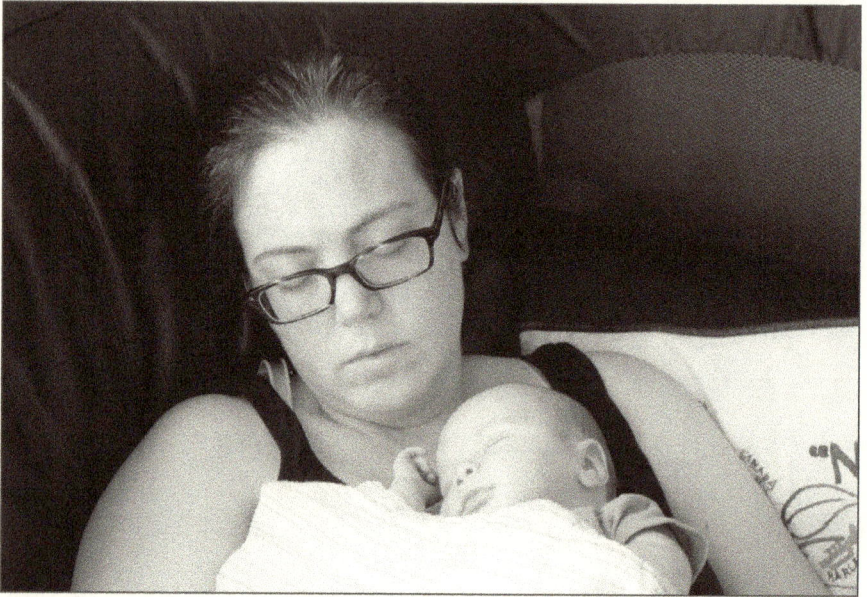

Posted in pics

Fine, she's cute.

Posted on June 4, 2012

Posted in pics

It's a cluster, all right.

Posted on June 5, 2012

The bebe is killing us with her new & worse-than-ever feeding schedule, which I understand may be called 'cluster feeding'. Here's how it goes:

Old way: eating, sleeping, pooping, and eating again.
New way: eating, whining, barfing, eating, pooping, whining.

This is a big negative for our quality of life. What's that you say? I left 'sleeping' off the new list? True. But so is she.

Posted in Uncategorized | 1 Reply

Dad, sleeping is so last month. None of the 2 month old babies sleep. Please try to keep up. Love,

- Lily

Moonlighting?

Posted on June 6, 2012

Not sure how, but this girl is filthy. Her hands look like she's been sneaking off to a machine shop or garage every night…all sorts of grime between her fingers. I've checked her for a Teamster's tattoo – none evident so far. I'm not ruling anything out though. Perhaps this is related to our biweekly bathing schedule?

Posted in Uncategorized

Already coming with the attitude

Posted on June 7, 2012

I see that my 99 problems differ in one important way from the 99 problems experienced by Ice-T (and later Jay-Z….hmmm…is it related to the hyphen somehow?…I'm lacking one….). Lily's throwing attitude like feces in the primate house. Poppin' off and commenting on your own blog?! Careful there, Miss Snippypants!

Posted in Uncategorized

We all have our El Guapo

Posted on June 8, 2012

In a way, all of us has an El Guapo to face. For some, shyness might be their El Guapo. For others, a lack of education might be their El Guapo. For us, El Guapo is a big, dangerous man who wants to kill us. But as sure as my name is Lucky Day, the people of Santa Poco can conquer their own personal El Guapo, who also happens to be *the actual* El Guapo! (thank you, Three Amigos!)

Lily is my El Guapo.

Lately, the swing has been my village-full-of-identically-dressed-villagers. In fact, it knocked her out around 6am today, allowing me to get my beauty rest on the couch. A victory for the people of Santa Poco!

Posted in Uncategorized

The beeb, using grownup furniture

Posted on June 9, 2012

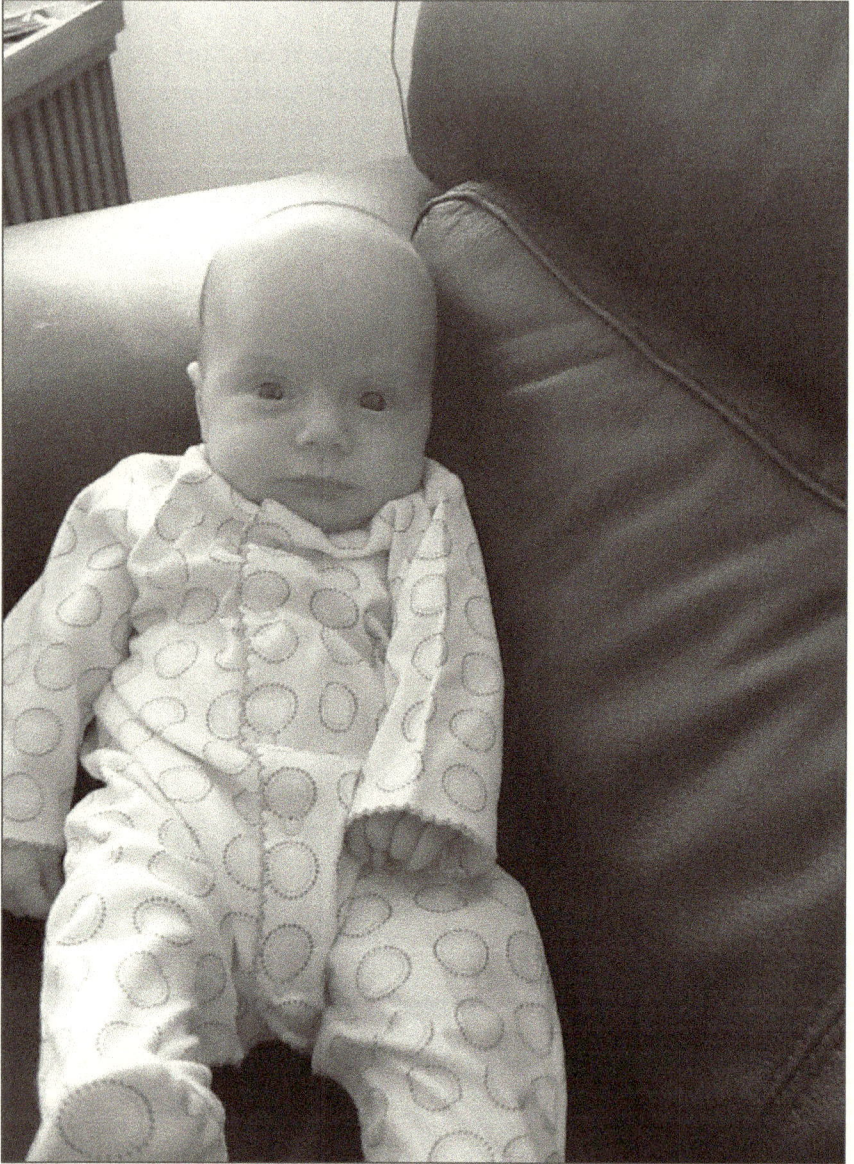

Posted in pics

How does she breathe?!

Posted on June 10, 2012

Nice mooger. That's right. Mooger. A milk booger. Can't get to it. We'll have to wait till the next nosesplosion.

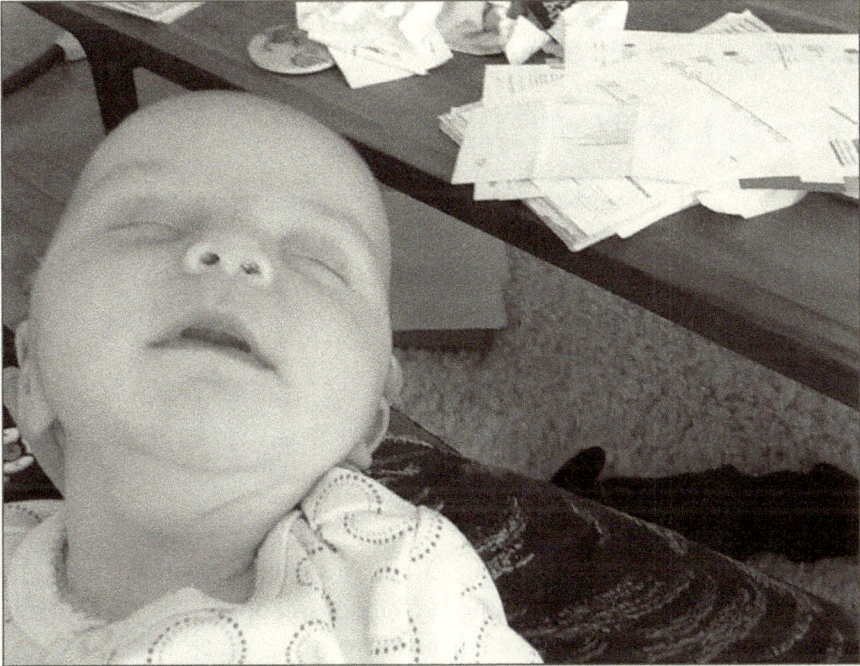

Although the mooger is hardly visible to the naked eye, its gravitational pull was detected by C.E.R.N. which predicts it will collapse in on itself creating a temporary fissure in spacetime. That fissure may allow barbarians from an alternate universe to invade our galaxy and eat us all. You are obligated as members of the human race to remove it any cost. For the sake of mankind.

- S Hawking

You can play along at home

Posted on June 11, 2012

I have invented 2 new games intended to engage the Beeb in some playtime. They're both fun and exciting and I encourage you to play them with your own kids. Or your coworkers. Or strangers on the bus. Especially "In your Grill". Hasbro has not yet returned my invitation for a board game rendition of either of these. Their loss.

Game #1: In your Grill!

In this game, I go nose-to-nose with Lily. Literally smash our noses together. Then I taunt her: "I'm in your grill! I'm right in your grill!" She looks shocked (best I can tell – can't really see her at that distance). That's the game. She's not old enough yet to muster a defense of any kind.

Winner: Me, by amusement.

Game #2: Slanket-Head

Highly technical, this one. I put Lily on a bunched-up slanket and then cover her up from toe to head (including going over the top of her head, although I do leave her face exposed). Then I call her "Slanket-Head" and attempt to hold a conversation with her. Maybe I'm channeling my inner George Kennedy (although he wrapped people in mullet in Cool Hand Luke…anyone?…anyone?…). My logic here is that the slanket is nice & soft and it must feel good against her male-pattern baldness. Lily looks alternately nonplussed or a little surprised.

Winner: Me, by somehow avoiding vomit on the slanket so far.

Posted in Uncategorized

Vibrochair out, Babycarrier in

Posted on June 12, 2012

Vibrochair appears to have lost its mojo for now. Shame, too – it's a good containment unit and has the advantage of being something you can put down and walk away from (while actively parenting from a distance, of course). But now she hates it.

Babycarrier is the new cure for all that ails you. It's hands-free, at least…but it does involve having the Beeb strapped to you. Not the right choice if you'll be wielding a chain saw or juggling knives or anything fun like that. It normally knocks her right the heck out though. Money! Unfortunately she sits a little too low to allow for a quick game of "In Your Grill".

I can sort of understand why she'd dig on Babycarrier. Who doesn't prefer to sleep in a sitting position with your face smashed against somebody's chest? Were I the child of, say…Dolly Parton circa 1975, I'd be all for it myself.

Posted in Uncategorized

Done

Posted on June 13, 2012

Bebus out. Evidently the walk to the French bakery with mom this morning was all she could take.

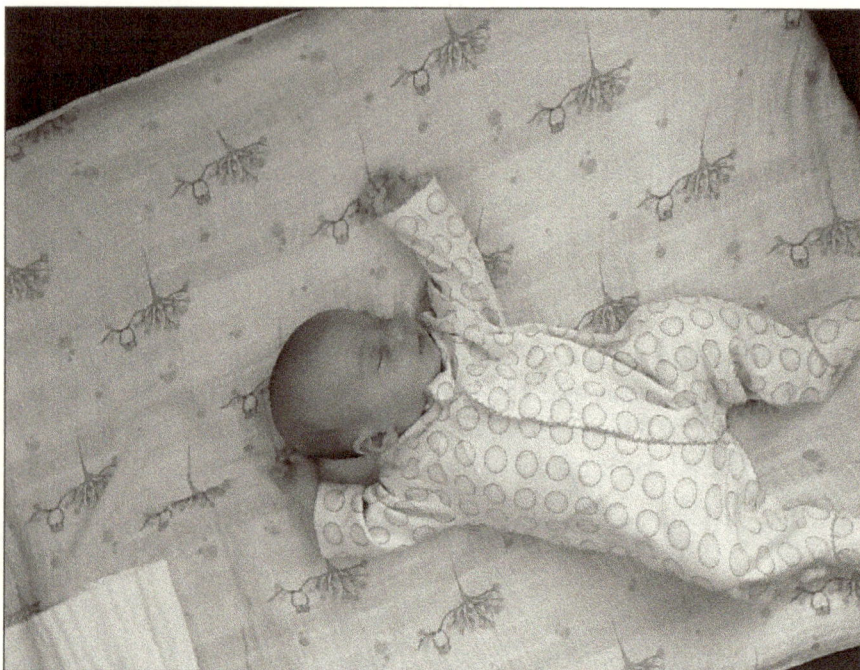

Posted in pics

43

Lovely doubly

Posted on June 14, 2012

8 lbs, 2 oz at today's two-month check up. That's precisely double her birth weight of 4 lbs, 1 oz. Whoo hoo! Well done Lily.

Posted in Uncategorized

Dude, that is freaky

Posted on June 15, 2012

So there's the bebe, straight sucking on a bottle. And her fontanelle is pulsing in and out…right out of some Ray Bradbury deal where she's gonna telekineese me across the room or something. Her friggin' brain is visibly throbbing. If she had thoughts, I would have seen them. Dude, that is freaky.

Posted in Uncategorized

The Traveler has arrived

Posted on June 16, 2012

Kinda looks like the Sta-Puft Marshmallow Man when she has her little hand caps on. I'm really diggin' on the concept of flaps on your sleeves that you can fold over. It's baby-specific in today's world, but why shouldn't I also benefit personally? Who wouldn't like a little foldover hand cap while watching a football game in the cold wind? Makes perfect sense to me. It's like you've taken your pocket and moved it out to your hand. Put the resource where the need is, right?! And who would forget his gloves? Not this guy.

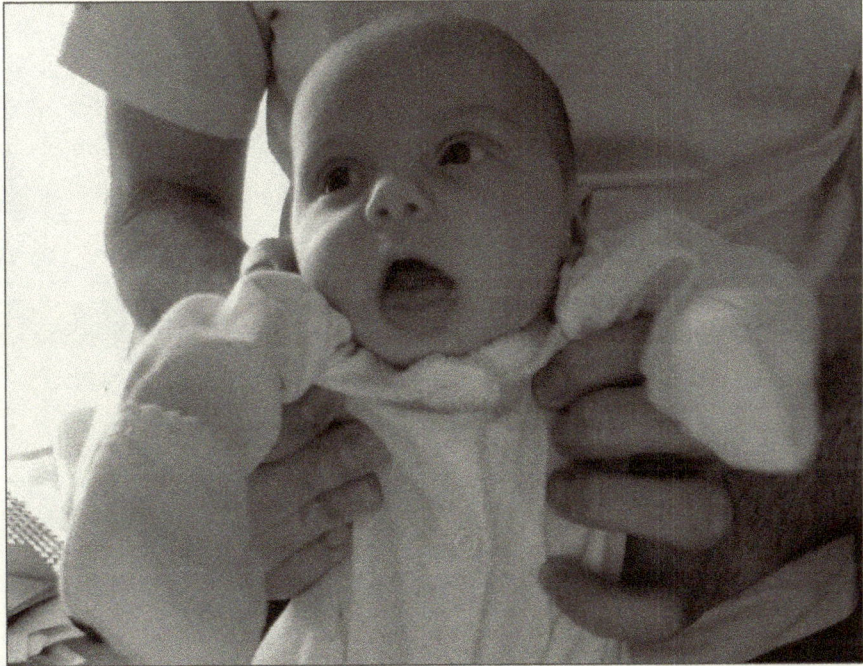

Posted in pics

Slanket-head on the NBA Playoffs

Posted on June 17, 2012

So, Slanket-head…who you got?…OKC or the Heat? Oh, yeah?
Interesting! Why? Oh…oh, really?… That is a mismatch at the
position when you look at their natural tendencies. What's that?
Really?! I had no idea. How long you been scouting them? That's
good insight. 6 games, huh? OK, OK. I'm sold. And who's the MVP
going to be? Of course. Based on your previous arguments, I don't
see how it could go down any other way. You are wise beyond your
years, Slanket-head. Wise, indeed.

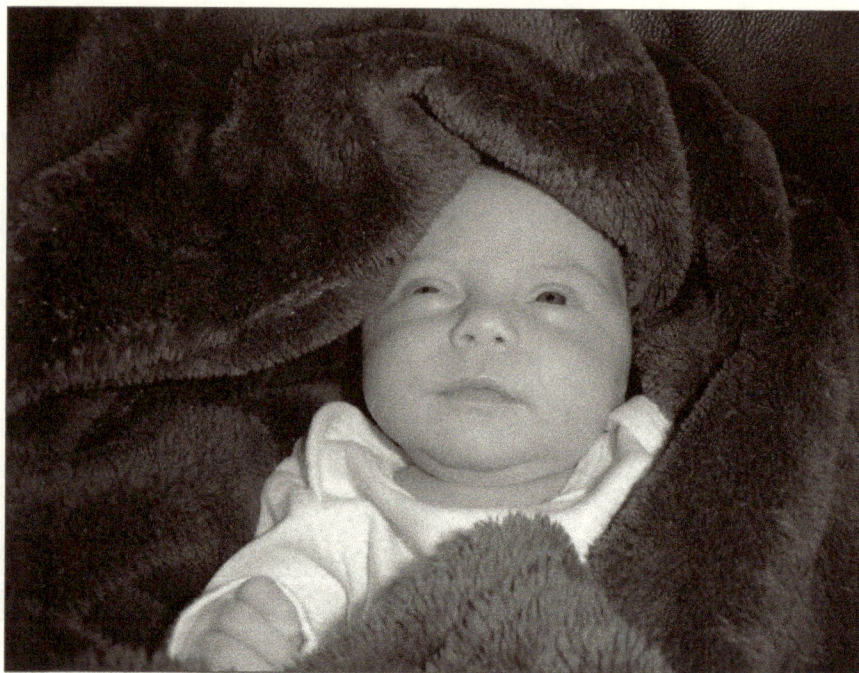

Posted in pics

Sounds like a rough one

Posted on June 18, 2012

I don't know what Lily's up to today, but I just received a semi-desperate email from the wife asking how early I could be home. I have some facts & information that are swirling around in my head…they add up to a rough day for Mom. Consider:

1. Kathy kindly took all the overnight feedings for me because I had a work obligation today that required me to be as close to full-strength as possible.

2. Lily's awake periods are becoming longer and more frequent.

3. Lily has greatly improved her lung capacity and the volume of her screaming.

4. Lily can be a right pain in the butt when she wants to be.

I suspect that I'll get home, open the door, and catch the beeb (who will have been chucked across the room by the lovely wife, metaphorically speaking). And I better get there soon.

Posted in Uncategorized

Lily smiles

Posted on June 19, 2012

She has figured us out. She can be a pain all day, and then she throws in one of these and we're toast. (She really is smiling, by the way, and no, I am not choking her.)

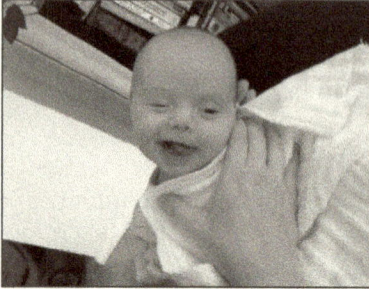

Photo credit: Christine C

Posted in pics | 2 Replies

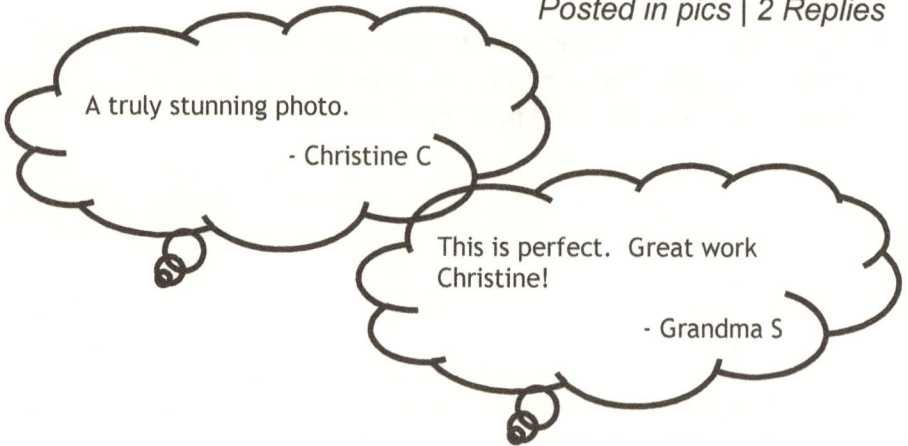

A truly stunning photo.

- Christine C

This is perfect. Great work Christine!

- Grandma S

49

Insights on spit-up

Posted on June 20, 2012

First: it's not puke. Puke is nasty and reeks of bile. Not so with spit-up.

Second: You discover it in different ways. Sometimes you hear it…she'll make a retching sound and that grabs your attention. That's not always the case though. Sometimes you hear it splat on the ground. She didn't make a sound. Sometimes you feel it…a wet sensation on your hand, arm, leg, or elsewhere. But not always – it's body temperature. So it may be on you and you're totally unaware of it. And of course you may see it, either dribbling lazily out of her mouth or launching in a graceful soundless arc. I don't know if you can taste it. I presume so but my curiosity hasn't gotten the better of me yet. It probably smells too but we don't let it sit around long enough to find out.

Third: It's a recipe for laundry. We're doing laundry at an alarming clip. And everything I own is covered in dry spit-up. Superlame.

Posted in Uncategorized

Growing vocabulary

Posted on June 21, 2012

Lily's vocabulary appears to be growing! To be clear, the number of things she can say has not changed. But I believe she's expanding the number of things she *means*. For example:

"My diaper needs changing" = "Waaaaaaaaa!"

"I'm hungry" = "Waaaaaaaaa!"

"I'm tired" = "Waaaaaaaaa!"

And as of yesterday, if we're correct: "Please put me down and leave me alone" = "Waaaaaaaaa!"

There are other, more complex thoughts she is expressing as well of course. In fact, we had a rather in depth discussion of the NBA Finals not too long ago (Lily was playing the role of Slanket-head at the time). I won't put the full text of her diatribe here for reasons of space, but the way she expressed it was classic Lily: "Waaaaaaaaa!"

Posted in Uncategorized

51

Powersleeping

Posted on June 22, 2012

The Hammer slept from 11pm until about 4:30 this morning. That's a solid effort for the Beeb! And it's having a noticeably positive effect on poor dad today. I say 'poor' because the previous night was not so enjoyable or pleasant. Not sure why she was able to do so well last night but we're not complaining. It might have something to do with her awakeness marathon earlier in the day. Thank goodness for the babycarrier…it saved our dinner on Sunday and knocked her out last night. I think quick walks 'round the block will soon become the norm at our Chateau.

Posted in Uncategorized

This close to some payback

Posted on June 23, 2012

Guess who's smiling and giggling these days? Yes, dad. Busted. But Lily is on board as well. So for all the diaper changes (she goes through 1 – 2 per feeding, with 8 – 10 feedings per day), for all the crying and whining, for all the jiggling and jostling and walking around to calm her down…..ma and I get: a giggle. Now and again. And a smile, less infrequently. Still not worth it, to be quite clear. But we're getting there.

I've heard that newborn animals tend to look like the father so that he recognizes the newbie and doesn't try to eat it. Same with the smiles and so forth…they're evolution's sucker-punch to keep the parents engaged. Because in fairness, without them we might eat her. Now that's not in the cards. I suppose I'll go get some sliced turkey. I don't want all these fixin's to go to waste.

Posted in Uncategorized

Cute but evil

Posted on June 24, 2012

Oh.

My.

God.

The Bebe went ballistic for a good 2 hours today. Would not stop screaming…the kind of screaming where she goes hoarse and gets all sweaty. Not a pretty scene. What's a desperate dad to do, you ask? Back in the carrier and we walk around the block until she passes out. Then you sit on the couch, terrified, hoping she'll stay asleep even though you stopped. What a sight I must have been…circling the block wearing a baby carrier…alternately whimpering and softly sobbing…leaving a pathetic trail of tears in my wake. She may be cute. But the Bebe is evil.

Posted in Uncategorized

Dammit.

Posted on June 25, 2012

Told you so.

There's a kid in the house. And I think it might be mine.

Posted on June 26, 2012

I continue to be amazed. As you can tell from the photo, she's not. I think maybe her primitive cave-beeb brain does not yet register how utterly bizarre this whole scene is. Mom gets it…we've discussed in detail. Her face resembles mine, only with significantly less facial hair and fewer wrinkles.

Posted in pics

Subtlety

Posted on June 27, 2012

It's all shades of gray in reading the Beeb. She has a thousand faces, of course....the classic poop-face, the newly minted happy-face, and of course the great-big-ol'-frowny face. Not to be confused with the face where she just sticks her lip out. Note the differences below. Just sticking the lip out:

Great-big-ol'-frowny-face:

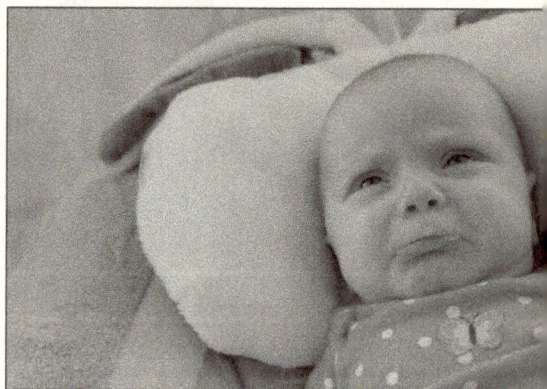

How someone can maintain that face when they're in a rabbit swing with floppy ears and everything is beyond me.

Posted in pics

57

Freaky-@ss cow in the house

Posted on June 28, 2012

Here's Lily with her friend the freaky-@ss cow. Or is it 'kow'? Not sure. But she had some fun with it today. It's destined to become a slobber reservoir over time. Looking forward to that! Note also that vibrochair is back in mix, courtesy of 4 new D-cells and the Bebe's ever-changing preferences.

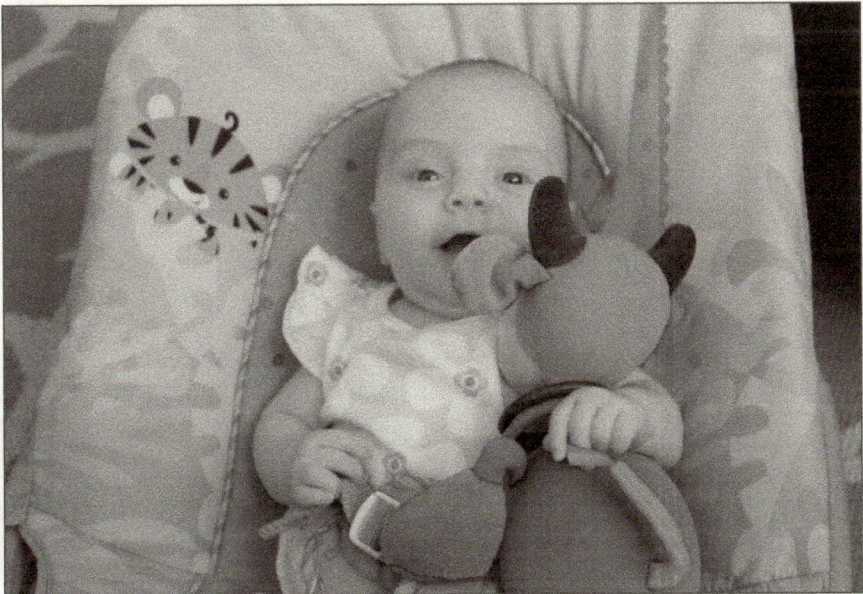

Posted in Meet the bebe

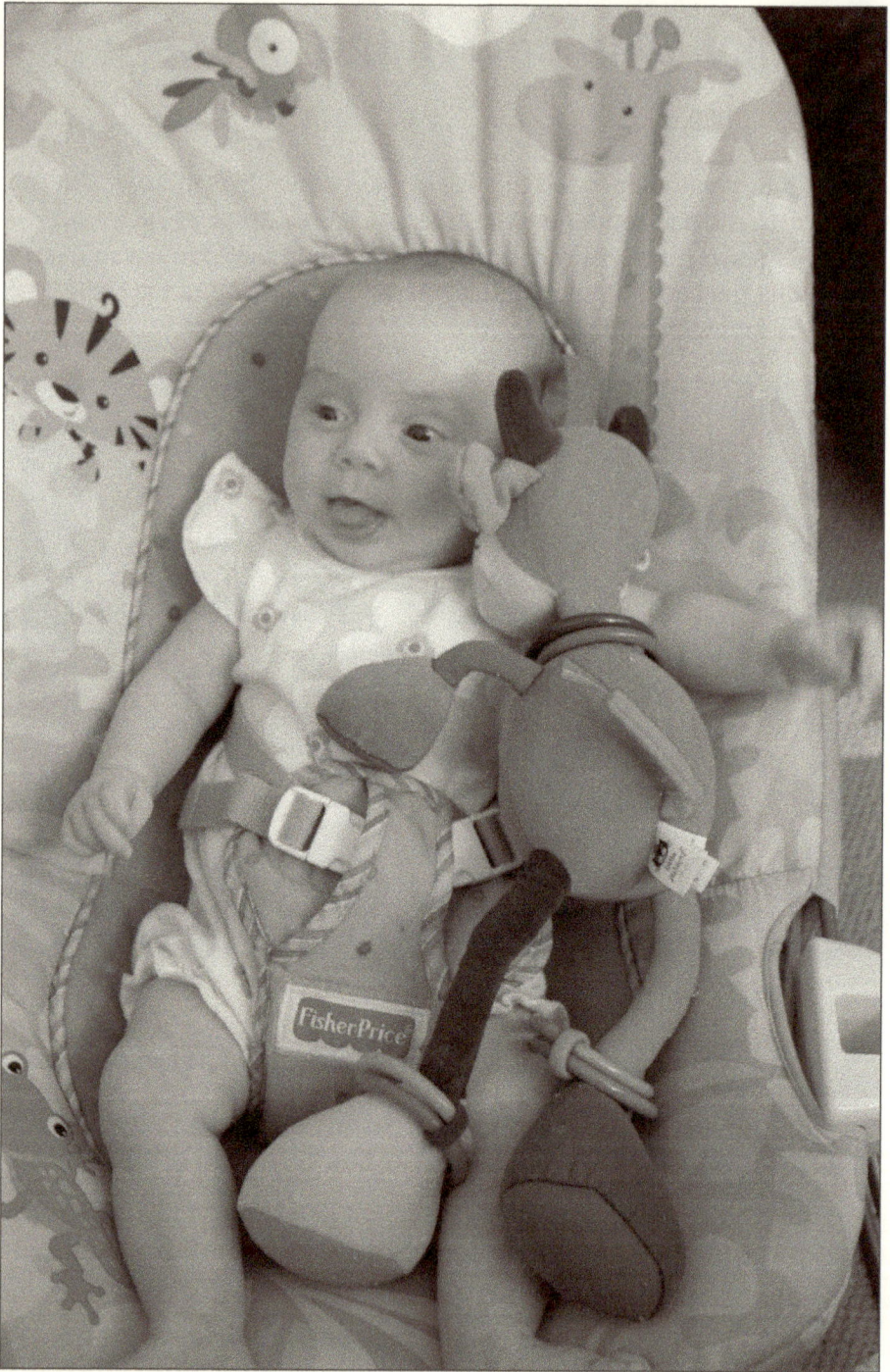

Gearing up for a flight

Posted on June 29, 2012

Well, not sure if this is a recipe for disaster or not, but we'll be packing up and trundling down to the airport for the first time. C'moooon Lily don't freak out! The best advice we've received so far:

1) Get her a seat. Even if you don't need it. You'll be glad to have the extra space. If nothing else, you can lay out a full bar on it for your own use.

2) Pacify 'Er. She gots to be sucking on something for changes in air pressure or else her eyes will pop out or something.

I don't know if the other brave souls on our flight have any indication that they'll be trapped in a largish steel tube with a bona fide Bebus or not. I doubt it. What joys surely await them all! As a recently childless person, I confess to muttering more than a little when I saw little babies getting on a plane near me. Aaaaaah, but the worm has now turned and the onus of parenthood hangs heavy upon me. Not sure I'm up to this. Stupid onus.

Posted in Uncategorized

Great success!

Posted on June 30, 2012

Well, all went well except the plane was delayed for undisclosed mechanical work and Typhoid Mary sat next to us in the waiting area. Actually, she was sitting 20 feet away when we first noticed that death-rattle of a cough. But she soon moved to be closer. Thanks. Then when we boarded, she took the seat in front of Kathy. When that proved to be too far away from the Bebus, Mary shifted that one extra seat to be directly in front of her. Again, thanks!

Posted in Uncategorized | 1 Reply

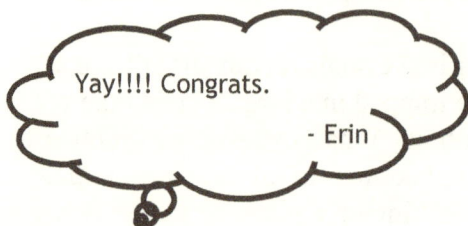

Yay!!!! Congrats.

- Erin

61

July

The bucket

Posted on July 2, 2012

Big take-away from the family reunion last week: referring to the car seat / bebus carrier as "The Bucket". I'm a big fan of the terminology and have already incorporated it into everyday usage. Sadly, Lily's not able to perceive oral threats yet...it does me no good to tell her that I'm gonna throw her in the bucket. She'll get there some day though. And threaten I shall!

Posted in Uncategorized

It's a bird, it's a plane

Posted on July 3, 2012

As previously rumored, yes…she can fly! Not in the Superman sense though. Or maybe she just hasn't showed us that talent yet. She looks more like this:

It's really just Lily in a car seat – not too much to the whole thing. But she's working that pacifier and sleeping peacefully, which makes her an airplane travel stud in my eyes.

Posted in pics

Fisherbeeb

Posted on July 5, 2012

In the midst of the family maelstrom, we did find a few minutes to go fishing and Lily was kind enough to join us. We experienced none of the usual first-time-fishing occurrences (I understand the top 5 are: fish hook through the ear, child in the water, fish wriggling out of your hands and tail slapping someone upside the head, child complaining that "you're hurting the fish", and persistent fish odor in car). Let's call it a success then, shall we? I hope she grows to enjoy some torture & release activities in the future. I do!

P.S. The only fish we saw swam over to us and then milled around in about 2 inches of water. It was a brook trout that was clearly not right in the head....old or sick or both. Sad really, but I made him my mascot and we hung out together.

Posted in pics

Primus knows all

Posted on July 6, 2012

I am beginning to suspect that we are living through the Primus album "Frizzle Fry". The following selections from that album are playing an active role in our lives:

1. "Pudding Time". The unofficial anthem of feedings. I am going for a Pavlovian response to the phrase but have not been successful so far.

2. "John the Fisherman". See previous post, Fisherbeeb. She's on track.

It could be argued that simply by having a child we have incorporated "Too Many Puppies". Well, Mr. Smartypants, that's a matter of opinion. And I don't appreciate your nasty commentary.

Posted in Uncategorized

Early dad failures

Posted on July 7, 2012

I have since learned that this is not the correct use of a onesie. My bad.

Top 5 Eagerly Anticipated Realizations

Posted on July 8, 2012

1. If I push my pacifier out of my mouth with my tongue, I will no longer be sucking on my pacifier.
2. I will be less hungry if I stop spitting up so much of what I eat. I will also be drier and slightly less sticky.
3. Waiting for a clean diaper to do a poo is just not cool.
4. Closely related to (3) above, waiting until dad is applying diaper rash cream to fart is similarly uncool.
5. Closely related to (1) above, my arms are attached to me and when I fling them against my pacifier, they remove the pacifier from my mouth, meaning that I am no longer sucking on my pacifier.

Posted in Uncategorized

Weigh-in

Posted on July 9, 2012

9 lbs, 10 oz at the 3-month checkup on Friday. I guess the double-in-size-every-month trend is already over. Kinda screws up my hopes for world domination with a BOUS (Bebus of Unusual Size). I guess they don't really exist. Doc said everything looks normal and so forth, so the plan is to keep feeding her and stuff and let it ride!

Posted in Uncategorized | 1 Reply

AWESOME!!!

- Grandma A

Mmmmmm.....hand.....

Posted on July 10, 2012

Lily wants to suck on her hands. I mean, a lot. She squirms and squeals and does everything in her power to get her hands into her mouth. It's kinda gross because they're always covered in grime & God-knows-what, but I'm not going to tell her that. We've heard that around this time, kids make the connection that they have some control over their limbs and that they are THEIR limbs. So maybe she's figuring that out and testing it with her mouth. Or maybe she tastes like barbecue sauce, hell, I don't know. It can't be stopped though, so I've decided to believe it's good & healthy and all that jazz. Enjoy your hand, Lily. At least until you get teeth.

Posted in Uncategorized

Multi-tasking

Posted on July 11, 2012

Now displaying signs of multi-tasking! Wow! This is truly an amazing set of developments….I didn't expect this kind of coordination until much much later. Examples:

The Coughart: Lily can cough & fart simultaneously. I think the cough is the trigger event here – seems the strain overloads the pressure system and causes the blowoff valve to be engaged. This is often coupled with a 'fumble', meaning it's not just a fart…I don't think she's coughrapping, but I am thankful she's wearing a diaper. Normally.

The Lye: A combo laugh & cry. I think we've all done this, mostly in conjunction with a 3 Stooges marathon and a couple quarts of beer. It is a little unique in the beeb's case because she doesn't laugh until she cries (as dad so often does), she actually laughs and cries at the same time. I don't know if she's laughing at herself for crying, or crying with joy that she's laughing, but either way it's quite a sight.

Posted in Uncategorized

Phoenix in the house

Posted on July 12, 2012

Steve and the beeb get to know each other. I think he's teaching her how to smile, and demonstrating that his watch could double as her belt in the event she becomes a world wrestling champion.

We got a second picture as well, this one a little closer up:

Look at those nice round thighs - hers, not his. Or both I guess.

- Grandma A

Frenchy le Havre speaks

Posted on July 13, 2012

Bonjour, bebous. I haf been watching you now for quat some taem. I must say – despat your American handicap you are veruy cuute. Your parents are eediots of course, typical American swain. The formula they put into your bottel ees an abomination that straikes at the heart of God heemself. Had you been born Franch, you would haf enjoyed the traditional bebous mixeur consisting of 1/3 unpasturize-ed milk, 1/3 red waine, and 1/3 Gruyere. Everything you would need for a laiftime of good health. Administer-ed as a suppository of course. It causses me pain, knowing what you must eat instead. I vow to aid you in resisting this dietary oppression if you can find your way to Fraonce. Be strong until then, mon Ami.

Posted in Uncategorized

Sensory overload

Posted on July 16, 2012

We felt it best to bombard the poor bebus with as many visual inputs as possible. You can see here that she is 1) engaged, 2) sitting in a bumbo seat with no assistance, and 3) scheming to take over the world (note the hand-wringing).

The hand-wringing is a bit of a problem, actually...she seems to have discovered her hands and will stop at nothing to get them into her mouth. Makes it difficult to deliver a bottle of whatever. Also means her hands are nasty, covered in drool and whatever she touches. Gross. Probably good for the immune system though.

Posted in pics | 1 Reply

Can't believe she's sitting up!!!! Those chairs are great.

- Grandma A

75

Flashback: Central Park

Posted on July 17, 2012

This was a couple months ago now, I think. Lily has me pinned. Her massive…uh….mass…being obviously too much for me to overcome. Maybe I was weakened by the plate of chocolate pie or cake or whatever it was (and whatever it was, it was delicious).

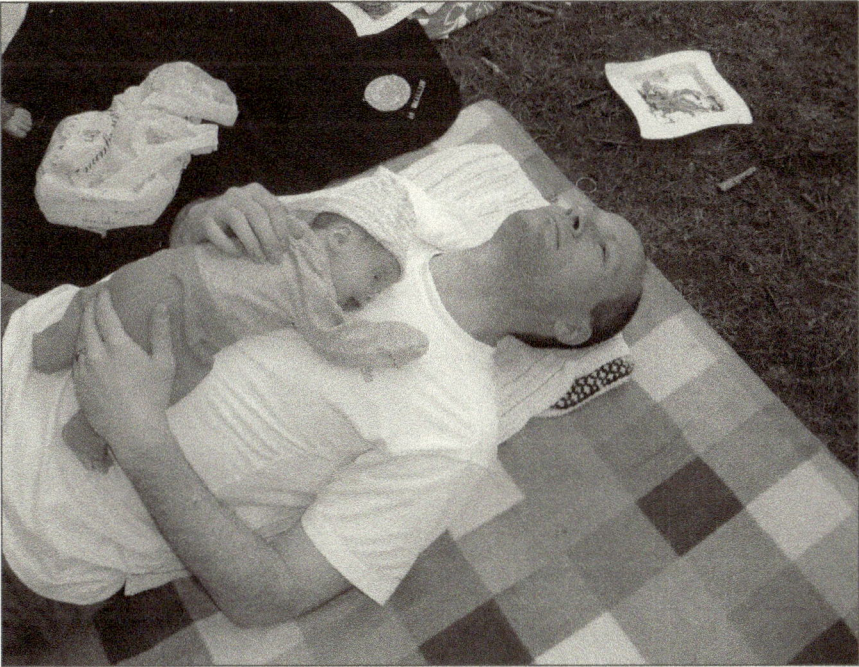

Posted in Flashback, pics

Mouth breather

Posted on July 18, 2012

She's a little sleeping angel, yes….but needs to learn to breathe through her nose. I mean, there could be mice running in and out of there for God's sake! Never mind the drool factor, which will come back and haunt her some day.

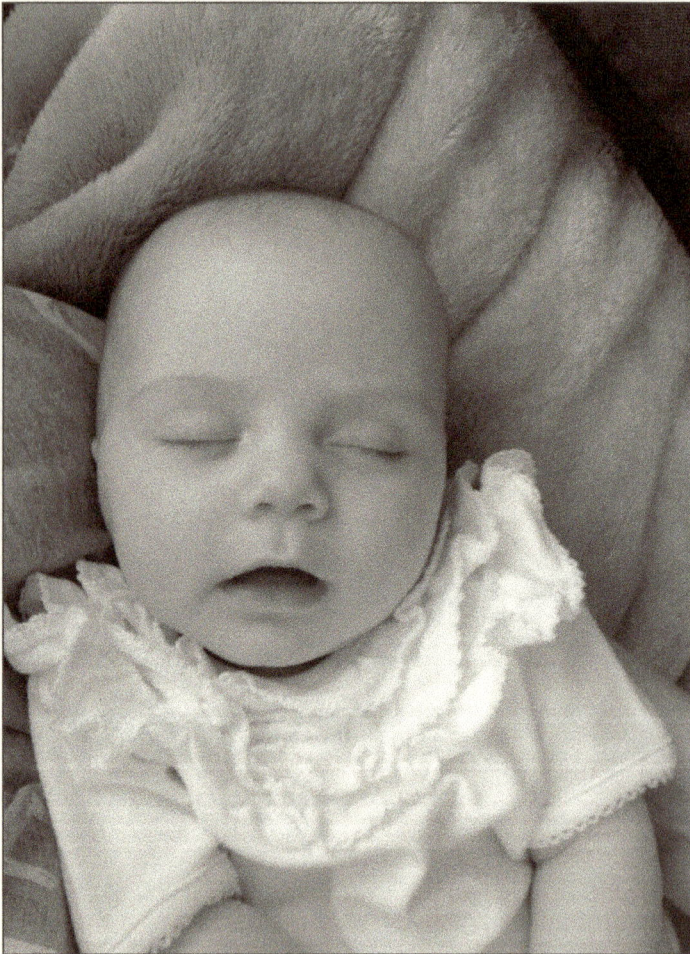

Nothing to see here

Posted on July 19, 2012

All quiet on the northeastern front. Lily's sleep patterns have changed for the worse again, but I think I complained about that already. Not sure. Maybe that was different. Allow me, then, to stretch out my complaining muscles and give it a whirl…

So she's waking up all the damn time again. Goes to bed between 8 and 9 generally, and that's all good. But she's only sleeping to 130ish most nights. And even though mom can get her up and down in 30 minutes, she's up again at 4. And then again shortly after 5. That's no good. Mom's looking a little frayed despite her superhuman efforts. Dad at least has the option of mainlining caffeine at work, free from concerns that it my find its way into his breast milk. My breast milk is pure, baybee…pure as the driven snow (in Phoenix in July).

The only small giveback is that her poopy diapers are much rarer than in the past. She has historically rewarded us with around a dozen each and every day, generous and giving little person that she is. Now we're down to a handful. Of instances, I mean. Not talking quantity or cleanup method here. Anyway, her previous approach was to wet the diaper, wait until you changed it, then immediately poop in the new one. She can't seem to muster that sneak attack any more, or has lost interest. Hallelujah.

On net, I think we're probably losing ground. I would estimate that I would be willing to change 15 poopy diapers in exchange for an hour of sleep. Since our sleep is down 2 hours or so and our poopy diaper count is down only 7 or 8, the math stacks up against us. I suppose this, too, shall pass. Meanwhile, off to poop my diaper…I'm not incontinent, mind…I just want to push the ratio a little.

Posted in Uncategorized

Intestinal gas, thou art mine nemesis

Posted on July 20, 2012

For the love of pete…it seems the Bebe's digestive tract is no longer happy with her diet. She's windy, as they said back in the day. That's fine and all (a rare time in a lady's life when she can fart loudly and often and everyone giggles), but it disrupts her fragile sleep cycle. She was up every 2 hours last night – it's like when she first came home from the hospital. A bad development indeed. I have honed my sleepwalking skills to a fine point, but that's not a skill I was looking to improve. Going to try to find some nap time today, although we're off to New Hope for a hootenanny with our other new parent friends. I think we run full bore until the motor pops (or the adrenaline is used up), and hope the bebe is tired from all the social activity. Not a great plan, but we're runnin' with it!

Posted in Uncategorized

79

Bulk delivery

Posted on July 21, 2012

And maybe the riddle of the windy Bebe is solved…she went nearly 48 hours without pooping this weekend. From Friday sometime until today. Highly unusual. And then she unleashed the hounds of hell in a diaper. Or someone mircowaved a jar of Jif and poured it in there. Just a foul soupy mess, the likes of which we had not previously seen. And not satisfied with a single serving, she went back for seconds an hour or so later. Not sure if this schedule is going to take – feedings became larger and less frequent for a while and we're hopeful they'll settle down that way. I suppose the unfeedings could do the same. If so, I'm investing in a good pair of overalls or a drysuit or something. And maybe a welder's mask.

Posted in Uncategorized

Breakfast at the bakery

Posted on July 22, 2012

Groovy sun hat + chin strap tied above the head = funky cowgirl look. Success!

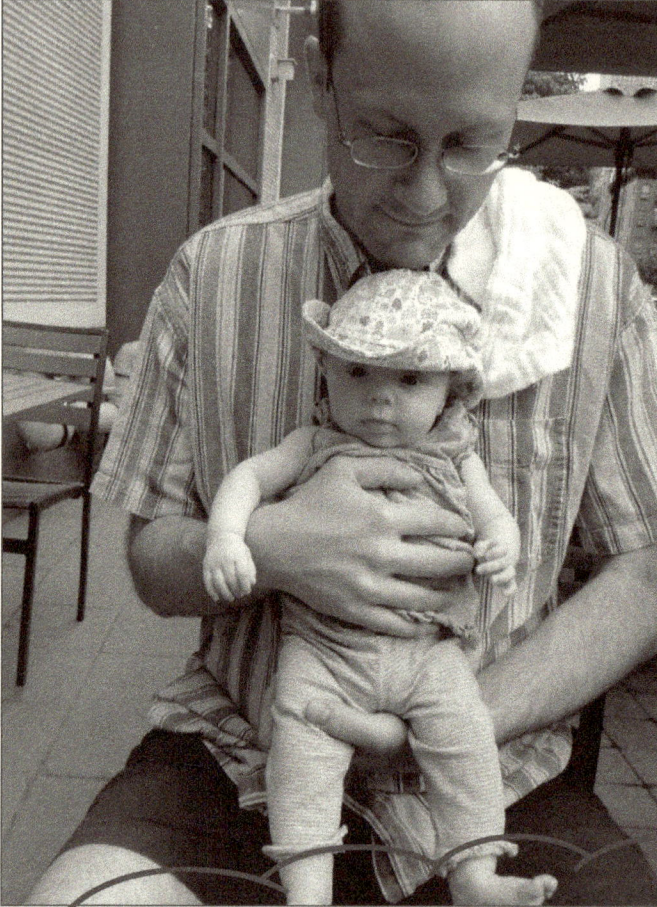

I love this pix! And the whole narrative above and below has me rolling and occasionally saying aloud to my neighboring companion, aka Uncle Scott, "Andy is fun-nee.'

- Aunt Ani

This is more of a Gilligan thing, except the belly hanging out. Note that means she has a belly. Success!

Time to bring in a pro

Posted on July 23, 2012

Well, we managed to find a nanny to help us through August…woohoo! I think all three of us will benefit greatly from having somebody around here who knows a little something about kids. Kathy and I have demonstrated beyond all doubt that our reservoir of knowledge is about ankle deep…and the beeb wants into the deep end!

Lily's had a decent day here. As a change of pace, we added the overhanging arch-o-playthings to our trusty buddy vibrochair. She dug that for a good 45 minutes. In fairness, it looks like fun to smack a parrot and trigger a barrage of lights and sounds. Like a slot machine, only no money and the arm is a parrot. Think I better patent that idea before Vegas thieves it.

Posted in Uncategorized

Preparing for war (sleep-training time!)

Posted on July 24, 2012

We're coming up against that magical point in time beyond which your child becomes sleep-training resistant. If we're going to have any hope of a bebus that consistently sleeps through the night, we need to act quickly and get a schedule in place. And oooooooooohhhhh booooooooyyyyy it ain't gonna be fun! The approach is pretty straightforward: go through a night-time routine, put her down around 8ish (a 'normal' bedtime), and then close the door and don't go back in until 4am. Easy in theory, but in practice we've heard it's water torture! 8 solid hours of listening to a wailing child and resisting the overwhelming urge to break in there and try to calm her down. Estimated timeline is 3 – 5 days if you stick to it.

We have assembled a band of merry men to assist us in the effort: Gma and Gpa will be up from DC and Klara the SuperHungarianNanny starts on Monday. The expectation is that Kathy and I will emerge frazzled, sleep starved, and looking like we spent a week in a washing machine before being beaten dry with a cricket bat. Lily may or may not have decided to adhere to a schedule…

Posted in Uncategorized

Chillaxin' in the crib

Posted on July 25, 2012

Lily diggin' on the mobile in the crib. Red, white, and black…those 3 colors appear to be the keys to happiness & attention for the beeb. Check out those hammy little legs too. Yesterday during tummy time (aka "Screamfest") she used 'em to roll herself from her tummy to her back. Neat stuff, but signals the beginning of a major change and a step toward mobility.

Posted in pics

Looking ahead

Posted on July 26, 2012

It occurs to me that eventually we'll need to give the Beeb some say in what we do as a family. I've been struggling with how much of a vote she gets, and when that vote kicks in. I think for now I've got it covered with the "PC Rule", defined thusly: Anyone who engages in regular pants-crapping gets no vote. This will exclude Lily from voting for the next couple years and our conundrum is solved. I recognize that it will some day exclude me from voting but I am prepared for that eventuality. Note the definition includes 'regular' so occasional PC activity is tolerated but will incur a penalty: a 24-hour suspension of voting privileges. Done. I think this rule could be adapted for wider usage, maybe even take to the political stage…it could be used, for example, to determine when elderly citizens are denied driver's licenses. Not saying that's going to be the best solution society can muster – just throwing out ideas here. Anyway, I declare the PC Rule to be in effect for the family until further notice or spousal veto.

Posted in Uncategorized | 1 Reply

"Regular" pants-crapping will be defined as 3 times or more per calendar week (measured Sunday-to-Sunday) for two consecutive weeks unless an exclusion applies, see below.

Exclusions to "Regular" pants-crapping are allowed for individuals who have a certified medical condition which caused the incidents in question. "Ad Hoc" pants-crapping will be defined as any frequency other than "Regular" as defined above. I'll update the rule book.

- Eddie "Guns"

"Cleanliness is not really an issue at this age"

Posted on July 27, 2012

"I don't know…today she pooped all over her own self. Up the back."

So went the exchange just now between Gramma A (asking the question) and mamma.

Parenthood continues to give and give!

Posted in Uncategorized

Gonna need a whole bag of Shhhh!

Posted on July 28, 2012

Boy, she is just yapping away nonstop! She's figured out that the mouth is more than just a milk-hole and the barrel of her barfzooka. We've gone from 0 to babbling over the short course of two days. Already she's learned to layer in some squeaking and a tactical eyebrow raising as well. Kinda reminds me of me…10 years ago and coming home from a trip to Automatic Slim's…

Posted in Videos | 1 Reply

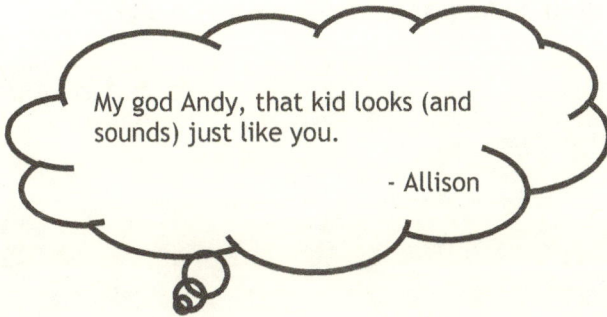

My god Andy, that kid looks (and sounds) just like you.

- Allison

Punt

Posted on July 29, 2012

We punted on sleep-training. Timing's just all wrong...we're going on vacation in a week and in all likelihood, whatever progress we made would just have been un-made on the road. So we bide our time and wait for now. We're growing increasingly desperate for it though. Overnight wake-ups are roughly an hourly occurrence. Ma and Pa have struck a deal on who gets to wrangle the beeb in the wee hours....anything before midnight goes to the old man. Anything after that goes to the old lady. Early morning is a judgement call for mom to make, based on the amount of sleep she's been able to secure. Two nights ago, it bit dad in the butt when Lily went nuts at 11:58. Last night mom got hosed when the sirens went off at 12:19. It's like war though...nobody really wins.

Posted in Uncategorized

Bath time

Posted on July 30, 2012

Working a regular bath into the mix now. Well…'bath' is a generous term for what happens. We throw her in the tub, splash around for a minute or so, and yank her the heck out. It's just to help establish a routine, you understand. And get her used to water. Perhaps most importantly, it's an excuse to use the blue Hippo Towel with her name embroidered across the back. My kingdom for a professional boxer to show up at a bout wearing one of these bad boys.

Never mind those clowns, the hippo queen looks like this:

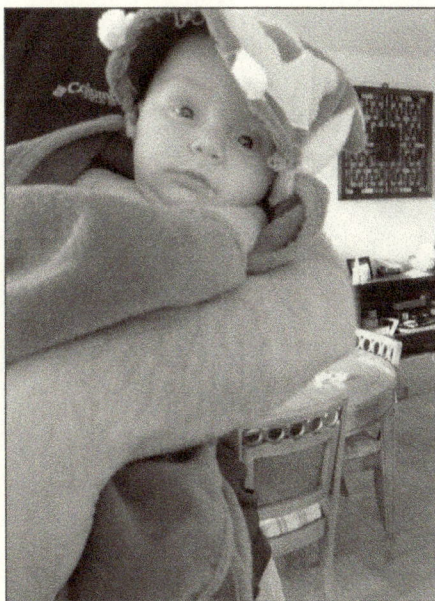

And this:

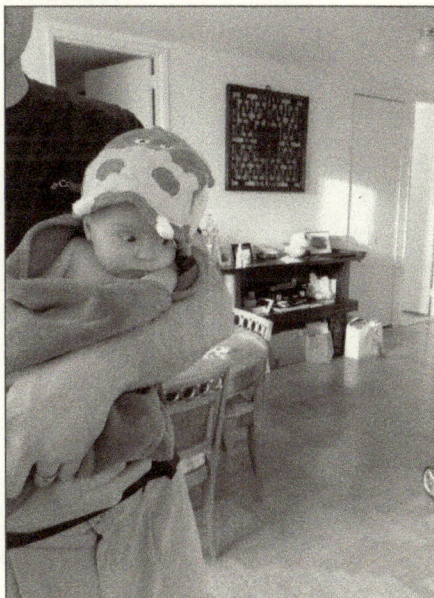

Posted in pics

Just another day in paradise

Posted on July 31, 2012

Nothing to report again today…we're in a minor holding pattern. It was a horribly unrestful night, and poor dad was working 3rd shift. Turns out that's not the answer, as mom wakes up every time the beeb does…regardless of whose turn it is. That means we were both on 3rd shift, making for a looooong and unproductive day. Klara the superhungarian nanny did most of the heavy lifting of course, but with two working adults in the house we've really got to hit a sleeping groove or our days of sanity are numbered.

Getting the keys to her first big plastic car:

Plotting world domination:

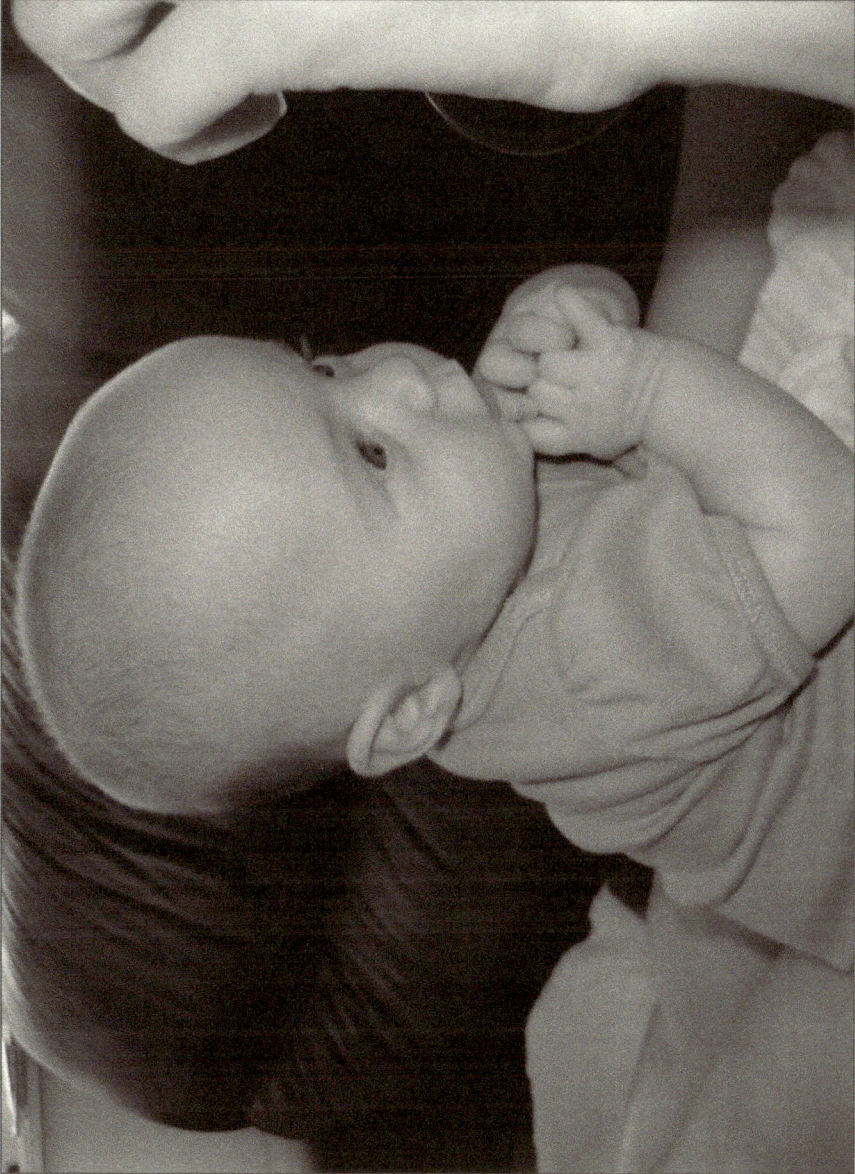

August

Terror in the box

Posted on August 1, 2012

Grandma and grandpa kindly brought a jack-in-the-box for us to play with. That's very generous and we certainly appreciate it…but it scares Kathy. She doesn't want to play with it at all, despite the fact that it's a pink pony with glitter hooves. Now, what little girl wouldn't be thrilled about a pink pony with glitter hooves?! *Glitter hooves!* Don't deny my bebus that thing even if it is evil. And I'm pretty sure it is.

Posted in Uncategorized | 2 Replies

I was just introduced to your fantastic blog and I am as happy as a pink pony with glitter hooves…GLITTER HOOVES!

- Serena

I wouldn't sleep with that thing in the room if I were you.

- Freddy Krueger

Nursery Rhymes Remembered

Posted on August 2, 2012

The hell-pony-in-the-box reminded me of the awesomeness of nursery rhymes. It plays the tune 'pop goes the weasel'. I googled that to find out what the heck the weasel was. Full story at this website, but short version is:

(English lyrics) Up and down the City road, In and out the Eagle, That's the way the money goes, Pop! goes the weasel.

"The Eagle" is a bar in London on City road. The "weasel" is cockney for coat (weasel & stoat = coat). "Pop" is cockney for pawning something. The point of the rhyme is that you were on a bender, blew all your money at a bar, ran out of dough, and had to pawn your coat. Why wouldn't you want to sing that to your little infant child?!

That's irresponsible, but not as terrifying as "Rock a Bye Baby" (in which you stick your child in the upper region of a tree, the wind blows, and the kid comes crashing to the ground), "Ring Around the Rosie" (in which we 'all fall down' dead from the plague despite our feeble attempts to ward it off with a pocket full of posies), or "London Bridge" (in which we as a society suffer a terrible collapse of our infrastructure).

Maybe none of this stuff is accurate, but I'll tell ya it makes me feel much better about softly singing the words to Iron Maiden songs when trying to put the bebus down.

Posted in Uncategorized

Going to Paul's

Posted on August 3, 2012

We spend altogether too much time these days discussing poor Lily's bathroom habits. Did she have a poopy diaper? When? Was she wet? Well, I'm tired of it. It's not cute…and it's a sad, sad day when you realize that 2/3 of your adult conversations revolve around someone else's entrails and the contents thereof.

Enter the Glade commercial. This was on the standard evening rotation when we were in London. It stars a cute little boy insisting that he be allowed to 'do a poo' at Paul's house (where the featured Glade product makes it a wonderful and rewarding experience). Aaaaah, the English!

From this point forward, don't ask me about whether or not the Bebe had a poopy diaper. Ask if she's been to Paul's. I'll know what you mean.

Posted in Uncategorized

Slankethead on Training Camp

Posted on August 5, 2012

So, slankethead.....tell me about the Steelers as we work though training camp. Hmmmm.... uh, huh. Yes, yes, that's true. He was the MVP, you're right, so maybe he's more important to the team's chemistry than Wallace anyway. Sucks if he gets away with no compensation though, right? What's that? Yeah....not much in the last several games of the year. He definitely front-loaded his season. Never mind all that, though – is the O-line going to be able to keep Big Ben's back off the grass? Mmmm hmmmmm. Yep. OK, I can see that. You think he's going to hold up though? Guy's been injured forever. But yeah, I take your point. What's that you say? Hold up there, slankethead, let's not get ahead of ourselves! I hope you're right though. We'll be in for a heck of a ride! Thanks for the insights as always!

Posted in pics

98

THAT's why you get a superhungarian* nanny

Posted on August 6, 2012

Quoth the nanny: "She just had a fart that the Russian army would be proud of!"
I couldn't make that up in a thousand years.

* Yes, she's originally from Superhungaria, which as you know was populated by Superhapsburgs until the Cossacks burned the villages and salted the earth in the mid 16th century (commonly known as 'The Laming' to most slavic peoples [not the Cossacks, who refer to it as 'that time we drank all that vodka and went kinda crazy for a while']).

Posted in Uncategorized

Mellow

Posted on August 7, 2012

You can't see her in this one, but trust me when I say Lily's enjoying this. We have a beautiful view of the harbor and plenty of space for running around. Bebe's don't run as you know, but the other kiddies can disperse and have a blast. There are secret hiding places and a fort…not to mention the standard dock, gazebo, outdoor chairs, and all that jazz. Ooooh, and a rope swing. Sweet! A few more days here and I'm going to be good as new.

Lily's babbling has not slowed down and being around other kids is clearly stimulating her. Good stuff!

[Ooops - I think the picture got lost, but a straight landscape version is posted at Which one's yours?]

Posted in Uncategorized | 1 Reply

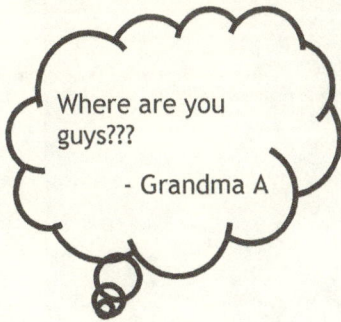

Where are you guys???

  - Grandma A

Cousin Hadley

Posted on August 8, 2012

We could not be any happier to welcome new cousin Hadley to the world! I look forward to a future bebe-off at Thanksgiving or some such family gathering. Congrats to Auntie Em and Uncle Russ! Here's a pic of Lily when we explained to her that she had a new family member to meet. Excited? Enthralled? Yes indeed!

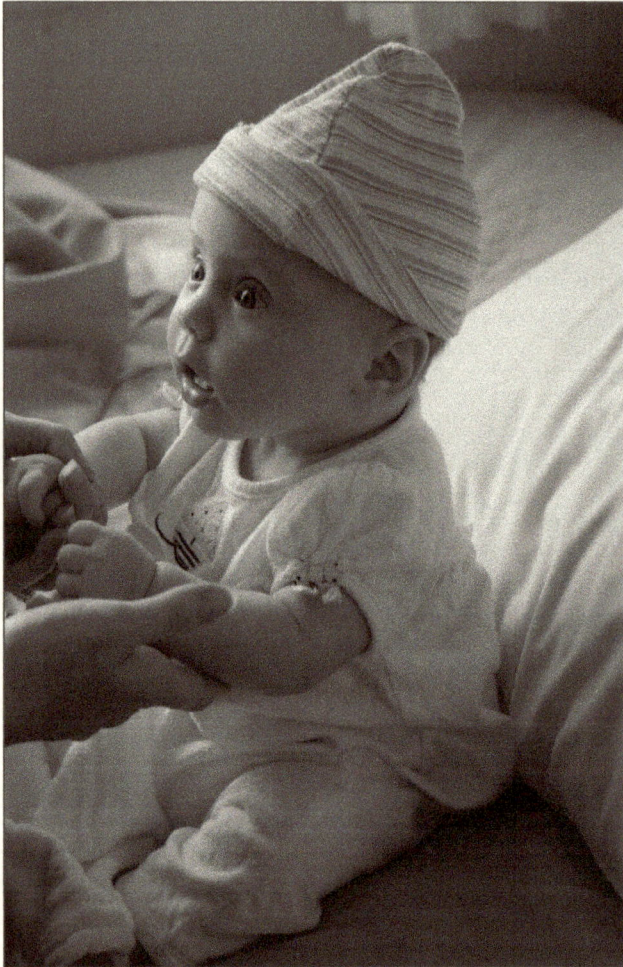

Posted in pics

Patty-cakes

Posted on August 10, 2012

Boy, did we have some fun with patty-cakes the other day. Lily got going with a solid belly laugh. It's a slow burn and it took a couple rounds to find it, but it's there. And it's really cute.

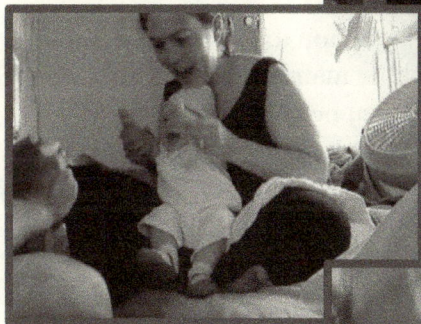

Posted in Videos

Thunderpants and the Code Brown

Posted on August 11, 2012

No, it's not a James Bond movie. And yeah, I know…more toilet humor that I thought we could avoid. But calling a little girl 'Thunderpants' is more fun than I anticipated. And thundery she continues to be.

'Code Brown' is just an alternate shorthand for a trip to Paul's. Makes you feel very official when you can announce that "We have a code brown on our hands! I repeat: we have a code brown!" I think supermarkets and other large stores have a similar phrase for similar situations which get out of hand and onto the floor. For them, it's a way to tell the lowest man on the totem pole to 1) grab the hazmat / bodily fluid cleanup kit and proceed to the scene of the crime, 2) question once again how much he needs this stupid job, and 3) stay in school.

I would be remiss if I neglected to mention the poogina. Poogina occurs when little Miss Lily somehow manages to go code brown in a forward direction. It seems to happen nearly every time. I generally shake my head slowly and in a fog of confusion wonder how I passed whatever health class it was where they taught female anatomy.

Posted in Uncategorized

Which one's yours?

Posted on August 12, 2012

Ma and Lily enjoying their respective bottles. I think Kathy's is the green one. This taken from Robinson's Wharf in Maine, where we spent the last week on vacation with some old friends.

We used lobster rolls and fried shrimp to raise our blood pressure, and the view from the porch to lower it back down again:

Room-a-zoom-zoom

Posted on August 13, 2012

About to skedaddle, 4/26/12. In the next photo, there is only a cloud of smoke and the hat twirling slowly in the air. Lily, meanwhile, has run completely off a cliff and is hovering in the air above the desert floor below. Fortunately for her, she doesn't understand gravity and therefore does not plummet to the ground.

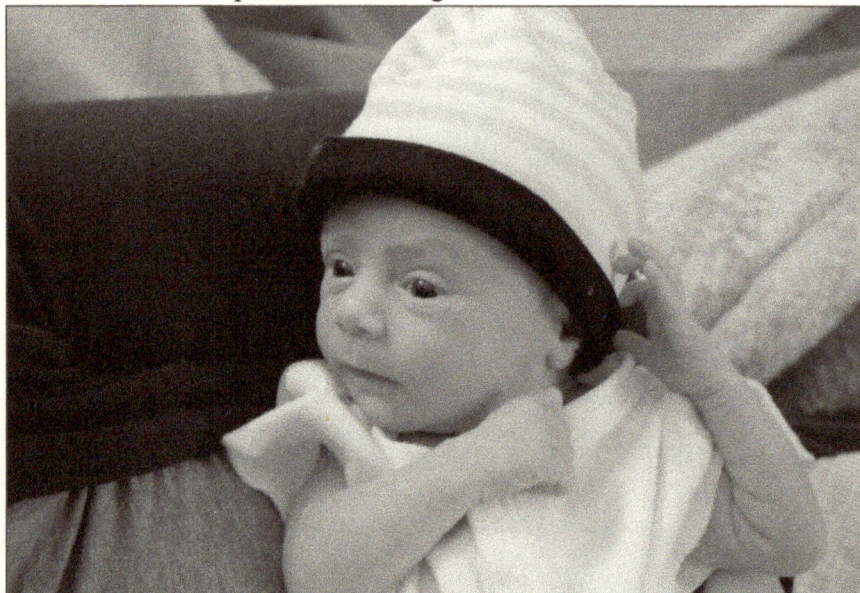

Posted in Flashback

105

Learning to enjoy the bath

Posted on August 14, 2012

Big milestone yesterday: Lily celebrated the now-routine bath time by whizzing in the tub. Faaaaantastic. As previously noted, she's a strong multi-tasker, and now we can add simultaneously cleaning and dirtying herself to the list of available options. Dilution is the solution, as they say, and I'm sure things were diluted enough that we made progress on a net basis. No matter....the flea dip, de-lousing powder, and a healthy coating of antibacterial 409 helped ensure we didn't send her to bed smelling bad.

Posted in Uncategorized

Nanny searching again

Posted on August 15, 2012

To be quite clear: Klara the superhungarian nanny is great. We'd be thrilled to have her full time. Sadly, she has a career to pursue and I'm afraid her time with us will end with August. The search is on for another beebwrangler to take over. Not a fun process as you might imagine, but it must be done…and quickly. I'm envisioning the type of transition you saw in tag-team wrestling circa 1986 – windmilling limbs and all. I need the new pro to come in like a spidermonkey and pick up where noble Klara will have left off. Tall order but we shall see it through.

Posted in Uncategorized

Infomercial

Posted on August 16, 2012

Are you tired of wasting your time at your job, with your family, or pursuing hobbies and crafts? Some people spend 20, 30, even 40 hours a week on these meaningless activities. And in today's frantic world, who has the time?

Try Watchin' the Bebe today!

Don't let your own life prevent you from reading about someone else's child! Start reading Watchin' the Bebe. Imagine where you could be if you *invested* your time reading this blog, instead of squandering it on boring everyday drudgery.

Our users report up to *minutes* of enjoyment from Watchin' the Bebe, sometimes spread across up to two days*. You won't get that at work!

Take charge of your time today with Watchin' the Bebe! Now 30% more self-indulgent!

*Results not typical. Your experience may vary.

Posted in pics

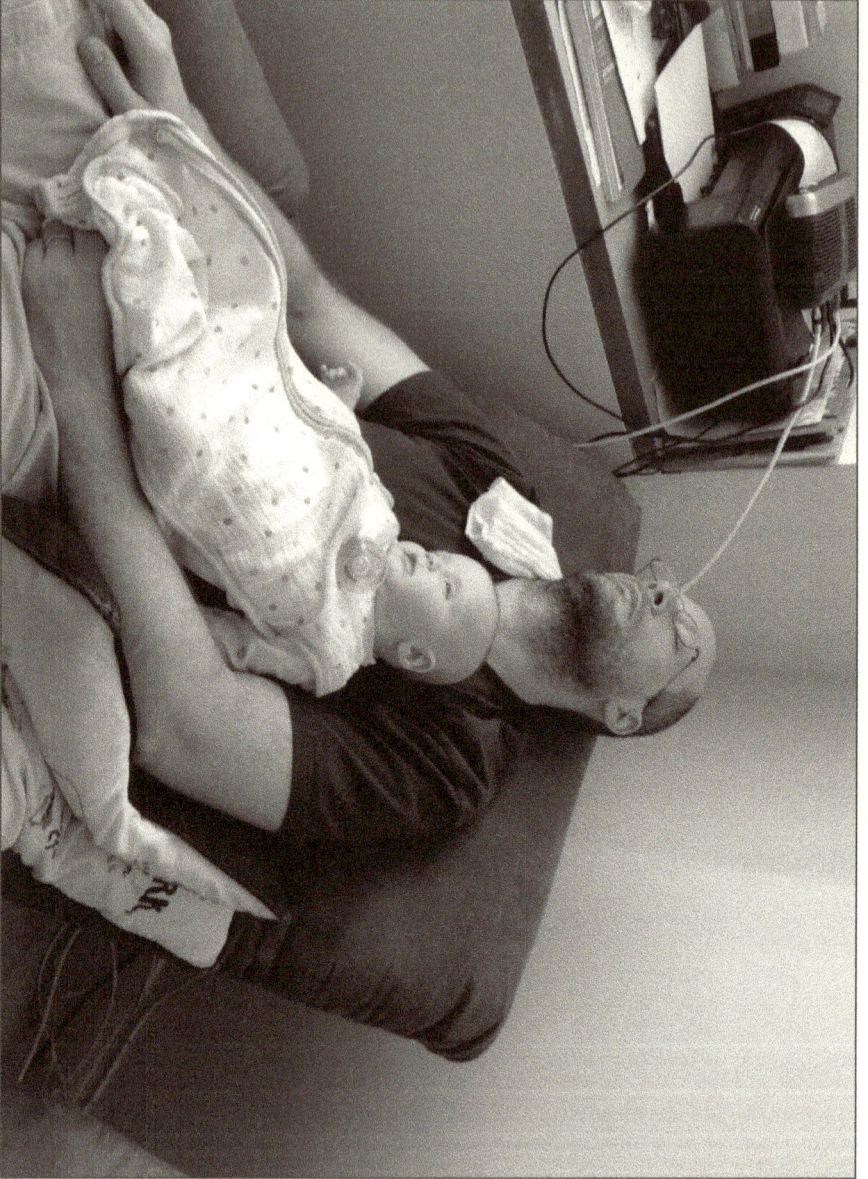

Weigh-in

Posted on August 18, 2012

11lbs, 6oz at the doc's on Friday. Not quite as big as we'd hoped, but a good showing by the Beeb. We celebrated with inoculations…3 shots and a mouthful of god-knows-what preventative juice. I think pertussis was in there somewhere, so she may whoop and she may cough…but never at the same time. Weirdly, a polio vaccine shortage means she gets that next time 'round. If she gets polio in the next 2 months, I'm suing the heck out of somebody.

Posted in Uncategorized

Target practice

Posted on August 19, 2012

I know I promised to stay away from the scat humor. I don't even find it that funny under normal circumstances. And every new parent has to deal with it, so it's not a big deal.

Then Lily Cleveland Steamed my wife at Target today.

Not a little trickle of poop out of the side of the diaper, mind. I'm talkin' a loaded-for-bear, both barrels at once, shock-and-awe level Event. The diaper didn't stand a chance. To approximate the effect, put one of those trigger-grip nozzles on the end of your garden hose and turn the water on. Hold the grip 6 inches from your chest, facing you. Put a kleenex over the end of the nozzle. That's the diaper. Now squeeze the handle. Pretend you're in Target and the water's poop.

I don't know what was most memorable to me....

Was it Kathy yelling through clenched teeth? "GET OVER HERE. NOW." How does one yell through clenched teeth?

Or was it the two old ladies who saw Lily, cooed at her, paused, recognized what was happening, and pulled a Nelson: (point) "Ha ha!"

I know not. But I know this: that situation was funny to everyone in the universe except my wife. 6 billion+ "likes", 1 very stern "dislike".

And me? I scooped up Turdzilla, grabbed the diaper bag, and then speedwalked to the men's room for the cleanup effort. Lucky day: this guy.

We didn't have a spare outfit for the Beeb, so she went home in a saucy toga made from the last remaining clean scrap of fabric we had available, a swaddle blanket. All 3 of us left crying very real tears. Lily's, of relief…she had been saving up for that moment since Thursday. Kathy's, of frustration I suspect, maybe embarrassment. Mine, pure joy. 6 billion people can't be wrong. Sorry honey.

Honestly, we were lucky. What better place to get shat upon than a Target? Right there at the end cap between aisles 6a and 6b. The display? Baby wipes, thank you. Fate smiled upon us after all.

Posted in Uncategorized | 2 Replies

^^^ LIKE! LIKE! A million times, LIKE!!

- Serena

That's my third code brown this week, jerk. I don't need this friggin' job any more. I'm going back to school in the fall.

- Target employee No. 5313874

Walking around the lake

Posted on August 20, 2012

Aaaaaah, little Lily enjoying some time outdoors. I'm diggin' on the hat. So's she. So's mom, by the look of it.

Later she fell asleep, evidently pondering something. Was she considering the nature of ducks and the rumor that their quacks don't echo? Was she trying to figure out how gills extract oxygen from water while our lungs pull it from air? Sadly, the truth will never be known.

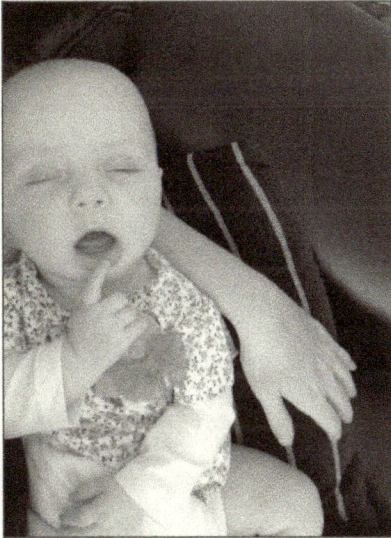

Here, I just think she looks a little like Ike Taylor (who by the way actually caught an interception in yesterday's preseason game).

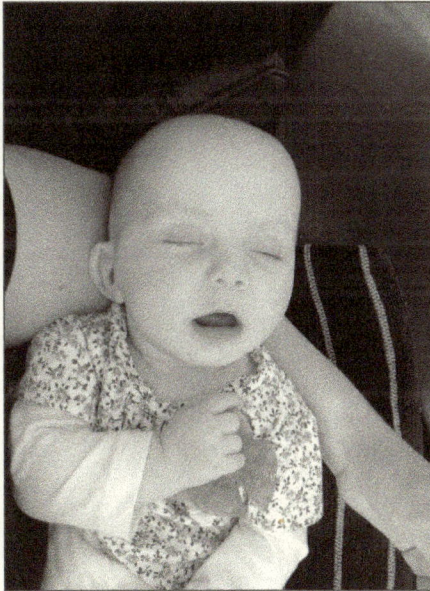

Thanks be to God she doesn't look like Brett Keisel.

You're doing it wrong

Posted on August 21, 2012

The beeb loves to suck on her thumb. But she hasn't figured out the traditional fist-with-thumb-extended technique yet. Instead, she goes with an open-hand approach that puts at least 2 and up to 4 fingers in her eyes. I've tried explaining it to her but to no avail. Yo, beeb: you're doing it wrong.

Posted in pics

I wouldn't wish that on anyone

Posted on August 22, 2012

Lazy people that we are, we had a housekeeper over tonight to assess our place and tell us how much it would cost to clean up after us. She seemed very nice, and was kind toward the beeb. In polite conversation, she let us know that she was one of 20 children by the same mother. Twenty. Ten boys and ten girls, all siblings from the same mother.

I don't have the foggiest notion how you would begin to care for that many kids. I suppose maybe by kid 10 or 12, you can start offloading parenting duties to the older ones. Still, 20 kids is a mindfreak to me. I presume it was in the days before Price Club and Costco and all that stuff as well. How did you buy groceries for them back in the day? One bushel of apples, a 50-pound burlap sack of potatoes, and maybe a pig? I mean, if you wanted chicken, you'd have to have maybe 4 of them. Four whole chickens, that's my official guess. And what if you went to KFC?…the biggest bucket wouldn't suffice. There is no combo meal for this situation.

I'm flabbergasted, and feeling rather weak at the notion that one miniscule bebus has us in a tailspin while others soak up 20 times the workload.

Posted in Uncategorized

Clean yourself

Posted on August 23, 2012

New trick: when the Bebus is drooling, covered in spit-up, or otherwise facially unclean, hand her a cloth. Her default reaction is to grab it and try to eat it. But she cannot eat a whole cloth. Instead, she winds up wiping her little face with it. It's a Huck Finn special without all that inconvenient time spent rafting uncomfortably down the Mississippi.

Posted in Uncategorized

117

Operation Nanny a success (we think)

Posted on August 24, 2012

Nanny acquired. We met last night with Natalie and she agreed to take over as Executive Vice President of Daytime Child Care, Development, and Protection. The business card is very impressive.

You never really know, but we're hopeful she'll be great. She has a certain calm air about her that our household could definitely benefit from. Strange thing, putting your bebus in the hands of a virtual stranger after a couple short conversations with her and her references. I suppose at some point you have to take a leap of faith and trust somebody. We're leaping.

Some facts you need to know about Natalie:

1. At the combine, she ran a 4.6 40 yard dash and benched 225 17 times. A PCL tear kept her from making the 53-man roster.

2. In the 80's, she was widely recognized as the "Haberdasher to the stars" in her native Trinidad.

3 . Before the operation, her name was Nathan.

4. She eats a handful of thumbtacks every week just to prove she can still do it.

5. She does not smoke.*

Welcome to the family, Natalie! We're delighted to have you!

*this claim not independently verified.

Posted in Uncategorized

Mom or Dad??

Posted on August 25, 2012

Either this is evidence that the beeb takes after her Dad and is learning to "squeeze the pig" thus making her unlikely to fumble said pig on third and short. Or she is learning to "eat the pig" and it just shows that she's a girl after her mom's heart, realizing at an early age that everything is better with bacon.

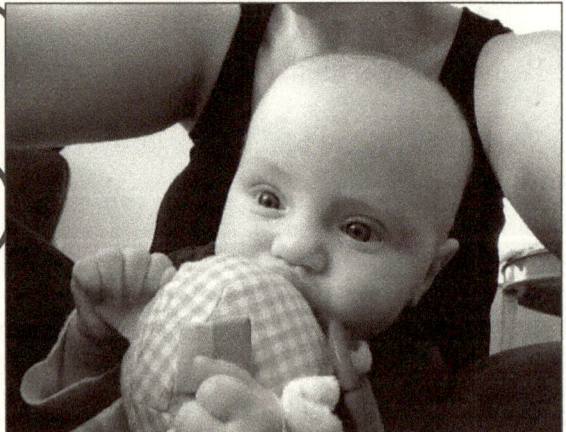

Ya gotta squoze the pig!

- Eddie "Guns"

Posted in Uncategorized

Why is she lost in the sheets?

Posted on August 26, 2012

I haven't done this for a while, but there was a time there when every time I woke up in the middle of the night….I was convinced the Beeb was lost in the sheets somewhere. I would get up (sleepwalking) and rummage through the sheets looking for her, believing it was necessary to make sure she wasn't lost or suffocating. I suppose this was triggered by her squeaking directly, or by her squeaking through the monitor so that I could hear her. Kathy would talk me into believing that the child was in the bassinet or crib where she was suppoda be. That would take me from sleepwalking to groggy and I would slowly, begrudgingly accept that it wasn't necessary to find the beeb in the sheets. And back to bed I went. Weird.

Posted in Uncategorized

Finding her voice

Posted on August 27, 2012

Well, we've "progressed" from simple babbling to other forms of oration. This morning little Lily was shrieking between 6 and 7. Some of the time, it looked like happiness. Some of the time, it looked like she was on the verge of a meltdown and letting us know. It was consistently loud though. This is the kind of thing that, as a non-parent, I thought was horribly obnoxious and terrible….particularly in a confined space (e.g. airplane, movie theater, or restaurant). I don't have any reason to believe she's going to be shrieking and squealing without purpose…hopefully this is just a step in the process of discovery where she learns how to communicate effectively with us. In other words, hopefully she gets over it quickly.

If however it emerges that shrieking is on the daily menu, we're going to have some stern words with her. It won't help, but I'll have to put on a show for others. Bummer that this started the week we're taking our longest family flight to date. I feel for the other poor souls on that plane if it turns into Shriekfest 2012. Better start planning my excuses now. Let's see…what lies can I throw out there to explain her behavior?

- She just saw Justin Bieber in the lounge.
- She's trying to shatter the crystal in first class – screw you, the 1%!
- That's her pedophile alert. Only pedophiles can hear it. Sicko.
- That's how she pops her ears.
- No, sir. I didn't hear anything. Stewardess? This man is hearing voices.

I'm investing in earplugs, just in case.

Posted in Uncategorized

Remember eating angrily?

Posted on August 28, 2012

Yep, here she is…or was on 4/17, eating and giving me a rather unsettling glare. I can't tell you why she'd be so mad at me. Seems I was providing her with sustenance and a warm, loving home. That look in her eye implies I was stomping on her feet or denying her voting rights or something. Hey, mellow out, Bebus. I'm trying to feed you this delicious bottle.

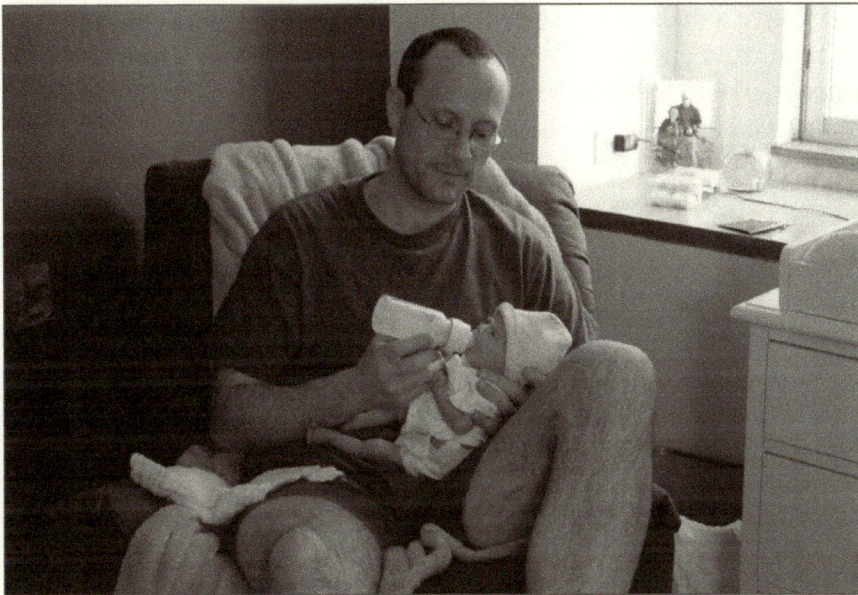

Posted in Flashback

Up and at 'em

Posted on August 29, 2012

Reveille was at 0530 hours today and the fetus formerly known as Sarge came out of the gates hot. As we slip into fall it's getting tougher and tougher to wake up on her schedule. It's still dark out, fer goodness sake. We made the best of it as always, with a trip to the mess hall and then some PT (a march around the block in parade formation). We conducted an inventory of our agricultural assets as assembled in the farmyard playset. Based on our intelligence, we may have a duck gap. We're fine for chickens (1), pigs (1), cows with mirrors on them (1), and horse blankets (1). I'm going to encourage the Sarge to consider herself on leave for the foreseeable future and let me sleep the heck in now and again.

Posted in Uncategorized

Lily in the morning

Posted on August 30, 2012

Dig these old man pants, pulled up well over the navel. She could mow the lawn in black socks and it would go great with this ensemble.

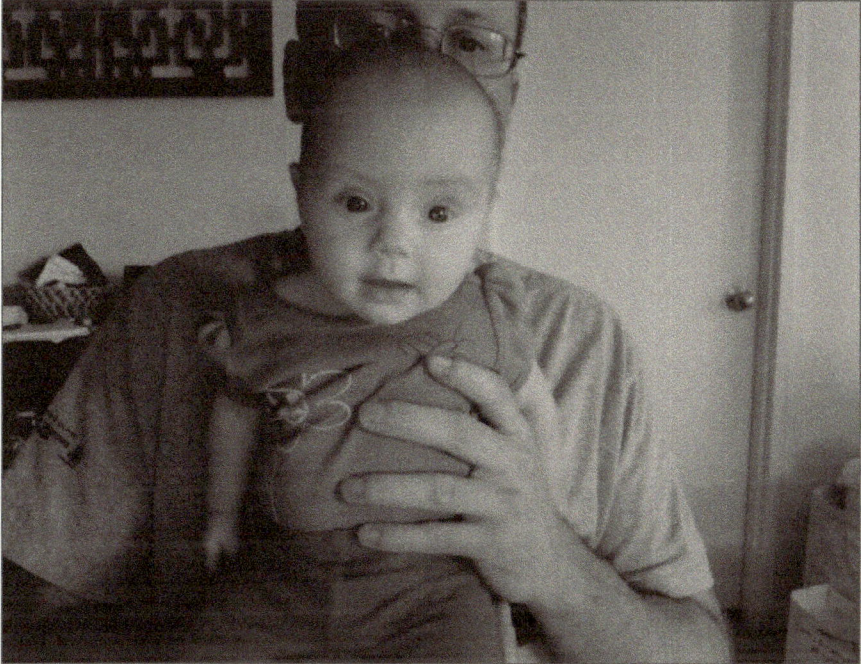

Posted in pics

September

Traveling Stud

Posted on September 1, 2012

So far so good with the travel. On Saturday we made it from Hell's Kitchen to Flagstaff by way of Newark and Phoenix and she did it all without complaining. Her approach to the flight was admirable…she used her underdeveloped feminine charm to woo those around her. How? Eye contact and a generous measure of babbling. That bought a lot of patience and secured the 'cute' label. That in turn offset the whining in the eyes of the wooed.

We've tested her resolve against environmental extremes. It was 111 degrees in Phoenix at around 1,000 feet elevation when we picked up the rental car and in the low 60's Sunday morning when we went for our sunrise walk at 7,000+ feet That's a solid 50 degree swing in 24 hours coupled with more than a mile of altitude change. Aside from cleaning out her GI pipes, we've noticed no real effects.

Next challenge: the time difference. She's pretty good at staying up late, but she's waking up several times overnight. And although I like watching the sunrise, I don't enjoy waiting for it to start before we set out…

Posted in Uncategorized

127

DC in the rental house

Posted on September 1, 2012

Auntie Ani, veteran of two beeb-like critters herself, spends a minute with Lily. Spawn of Ani (cousins Marlie and Jacob) are teaching the junior member of the crew some useful skills....yesterday Jacob demonstrated how to store avocado in one's nostrils until the time has come to eat it. Sorta like keistering, but in this case the storage vessel is nasal and the contraband is just food.

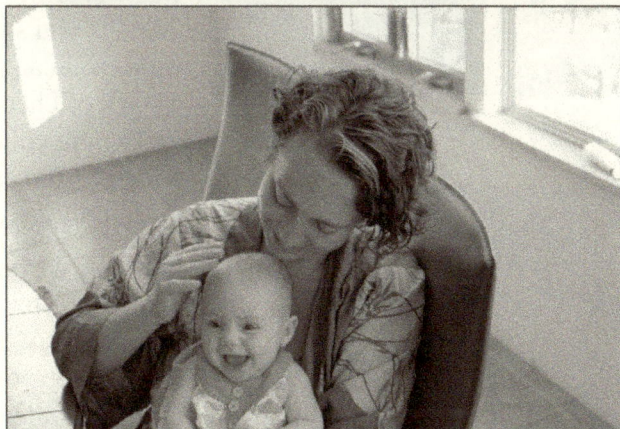

Posted in Meet the bebe

128

One for the anals of history

Posted on September 2, 2012

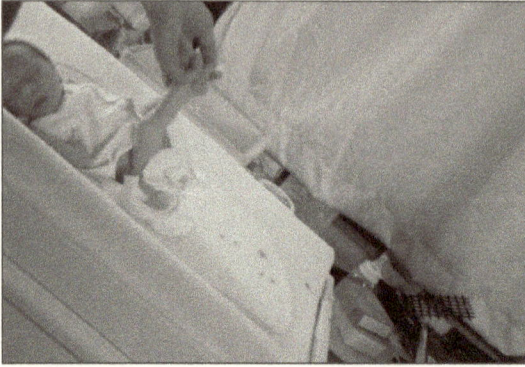

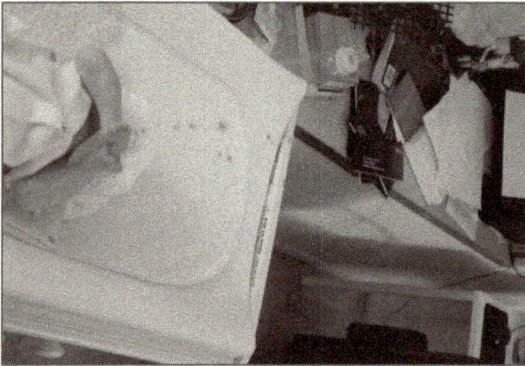

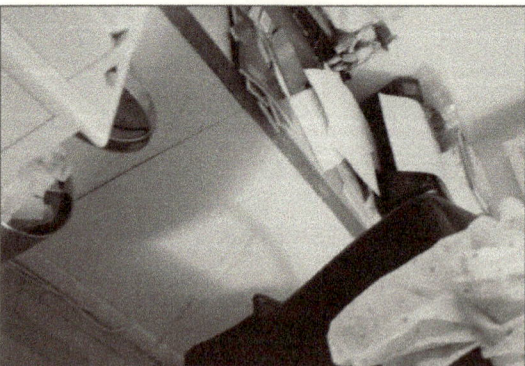

Yeah, that's right. And no, I didn't misspell it. We couldn't let this sequence of photos languish on a hard drive somewhere. These were taken 4/29. The situation: during an otherwise unremarkable diaper change, the Beeb loaded up and fired a sickening volley westward. The ordinance cleared the changing table and struck the wall. There was…ahem…*staining*.

And if you squint just right, you can see that a stack of checkbooks took some collateral damage. Excessively unfriendly fire.

In order, we have: the perpetrator herself, a point-of-view look at the vantage point, and lastly the damage done.

129

Confronted later by the paparazzi, Lily was shy and reclusive. We'll never be the same. The horror. The horror.

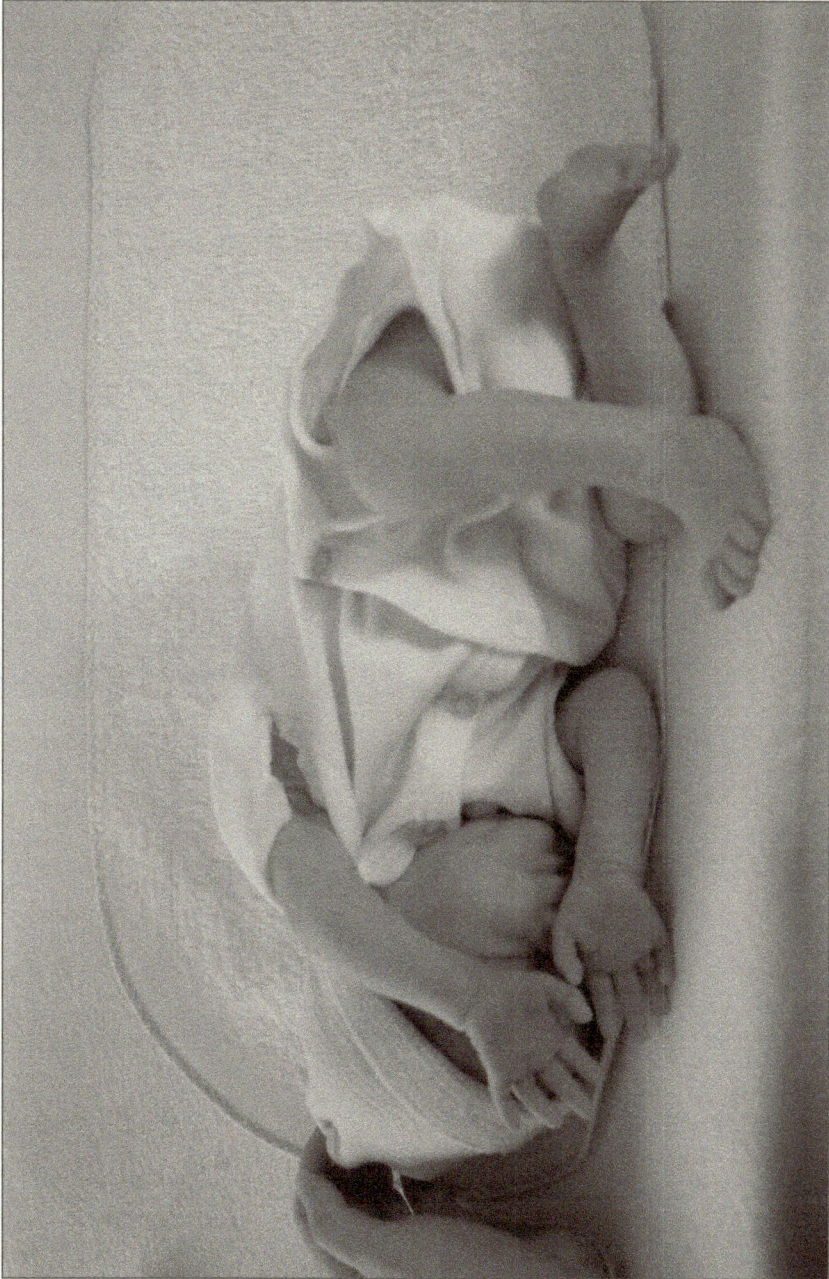

Posted in Flashback

Getting into a hiking mood

Posted on September 3, 2012

Here we are on the trail – Margs Draw. We thought this would be a good introduction and allow us to work on our collective technique before attempting anything more challenging. Between the hat, the sun outfit, and a 1/4" layer of sunscreen on all her exposed bits, we believe the Beeb was unscathed by the brutal desert sun.

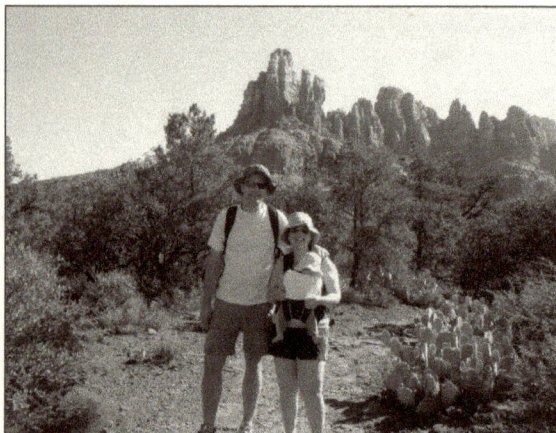

Here is the little girl dining al fresco. She didn't seem to mind the peace and quiet and later fell asleep on the return walk.

Posted in pics

131

Holding the bottle, no foolin' this time

Posted on September 4, 2012

Closing in on the coveted ability to feed her little beeb self. That's all good by me. This isn't a trick of the camera or other tomfoolery, but an actual instance of holding & eating. Atta girl!

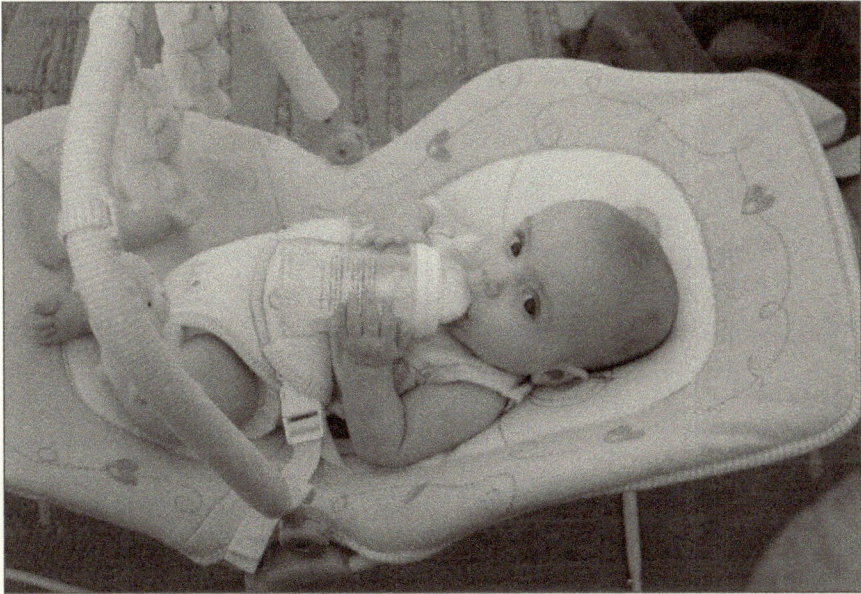

Posted in pics

Arts & Crafts

Posted on September 5, 2012

Lily found time to play with the cousin's buddha board. She's not quite coordinated enough to handle a paint brush (choosing instead to bonk herself forcefully on the head with it), but the fingerpainting action was a success. I don't know if she was attempting to sign her work with spit, or if she was going to eat it as part of a larger performance…she declined to explain her actions any further than required. I can respect that.

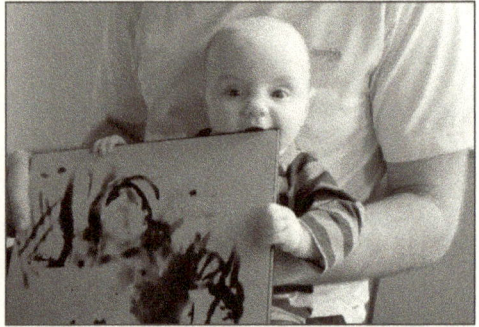

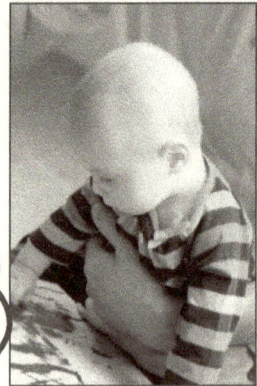

Dig the bonus bohemian duds. Is that from a thrift store? Or stolen?

- B Weir

This doesn't have anything to do with the art thing, but it's really friggin' cute and needs to be included.

Well, that's unsettling

Posted on September 6, 2012

Big night for us yesterday. Now that the circus has left town, we thought we'd put Miss Lily in her own room all the way over on the other side of the house. Nothing too special about that really....she has her own room in our apartment. Still, somehow the extra distance (50 feet instead of 15) felt considerable. Perhaps more to the point, we've been living in a scaled-down wild kingdom for the last week. Evicted from the vacation home so far: a bark scorpion (perhaps a stowaway from Phoenix) and a spider with a wingspan bigger than my palm. Papa decided it was a good idea to give her new room a once over with some furniture moving and some vacuuming in some out-of-the-way places. All silly, as it turns out…I found one harmless little spider and sucked his tiny self up. Done and done. What were we thinking? Hyper sensitive hover parents.

Then I had to go get my glasses from the car, and on a whim I took a quick stroll around the garage to assess the critter quotient. Living in the corner is a beautiful black widow spider. Odds of it ever hurting anyone that doesn't intentionally make a mess of its web: darn near zero. But we can't leave it there and must do battle with it later today. Like knights of old, we will dress in metal garb (fang-resistant tin foil) and arm ourselves with spray poisons for the duel. I'd be happier if we could relocate the beast, but homey don't like spiders and that one's nasty.

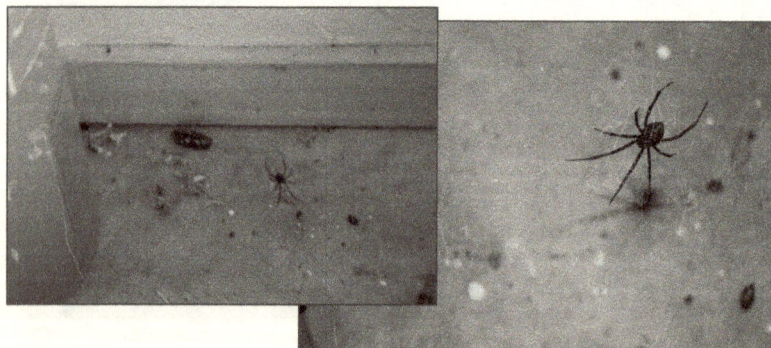

Posted in pics

135

Four limb tango

Posted on September 7, 2012

Displaying her developing powers of coordination, the Beeb can now employ her arms and legs in a synchronized fashion. Here's how it goes: she'll be playing with something and drop it….it will settle by her legs (either on the end of a tether like our good friend Ladybug or unfettered like our other buddy Crinkleball)…and she will use her legs to move it upward so that she can grab it with her little hands. Not bad, eh?! I think that's doubly true when you consider that she hasn't entirely mastered the concept of elbows yet. I mean, she bends 'em once something is in her grasp and she wants it in her gob*. But if you put something closer than exactly arms reach away, she doesn't know how to bend her elbows so that her hands contact it and not her forearms. Anyway, back to the point: she's like a little half an octopus with her four useful limbs. She also occasionally inks in the tub if you know what I mean.

The aforementioned leg-lifting motion contributes to her daily abdominal workout, which I estimate at around 5,000 crunches per 24-hour period. Anytime you put her on her back, she's got both legs up in the air for one reason or another. Once she learns how to use a spoon, she'll be playing the washboards on her abs of steel.

* Reminder to self: 'Gob' is a somewhat harsh term for mouth, a piece of information which provides considerable insight into the name of the candy 'Gobstopper'. Must've been invented by a desperate parent back in the day.

Posted in Uncategorized

Cast members

Posted on September 7, 2012

We had a great time with the circus in town. Here's a commemorative shot of the entire cast of carnies. In alphabetical order (note: does not match order of photo): Bearded Lady, Boy Raised by Wolves, Carnival Barker, Clown, Conjoined Twin, Lion Tamer, Muscle Guy in Leopardskin Outfit, Pickpocket, Sword Swallower, Ticket Booth Operator, Trapeze Artist. I think it's pretty obvious who is who.

I kid, I kid. We were absolutely thrilled to have everyone make the trip and spend a little quality time with us. Anything less would have been horribly disappointing.

Posted in pics

Vortexing

Posted on September 8, 2012

At Red Rock Crossing. Although I'm not convinced we got to the center of the vortex, the bebus has her legs poised to surf some spiritual energy wave. That same wave has somehow caused the lower half of my body to become disproporationately large compared to the upper half (as seen below). Must be the feminine energy. I only wish it was more permanent.

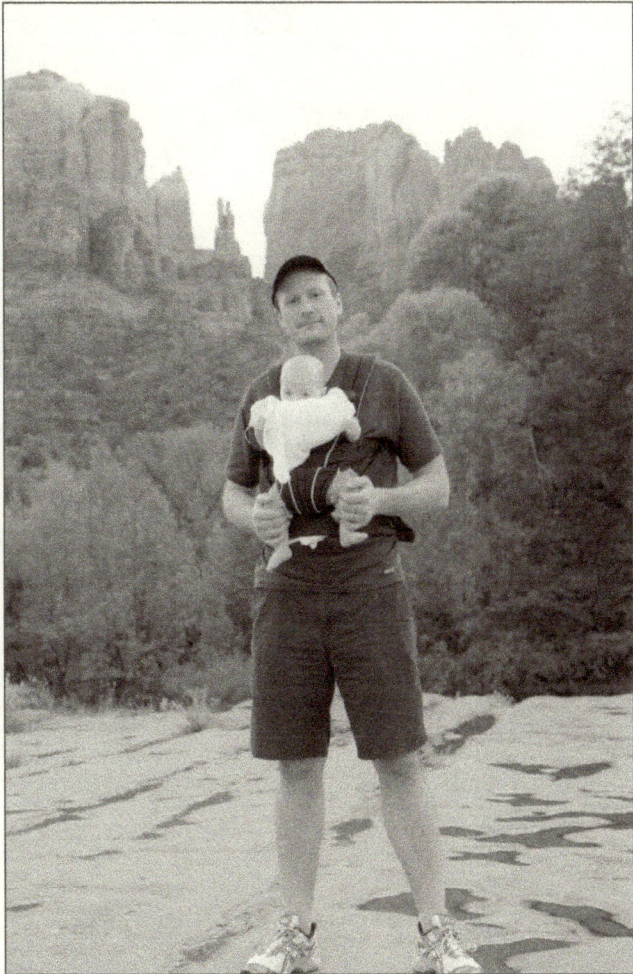

Posted in pics

138

Ain't that sweet?

Posted on September 9, 2012

Napping on the couch after a longish day. Even the bunny on Lily's shirt is dozing happily.

Posted in pics

139

Auditioning

Posted on September 10, 2012

The bebe is working not only on verbal skills, but communication in general. Here, she is reacting to a brown M&M found in her bowl. That's expressly forbidden in clause 4.3.5.9 of the rider to the contract and she's reminding mom to be more thorough next time. No wait…maybe this is the one where she's auditioning for the role of a tyrannical dictator barking demands at her underlings and/or railing against her opponents in an act of pure defiance. I can't remember.

If it was the acting thing, then this next one was an audition to fill Boris Karloff's shoes. Braaaaaains!

In that first photo, it looks like Mom is going to give her the "Holyfield Treatment" I invented.

- Miguel Tyson

Posted in pics | 1 Reply

Tonto Natural Bridge

Posted on September 11, 2012

....located between Pine and Payson, AZ. Gorgeous territory. You can't see it in the photo of course, but Lily's actually velcroed to my chest and not in the bebus carrier at all. I find it's easier to pose her that way.

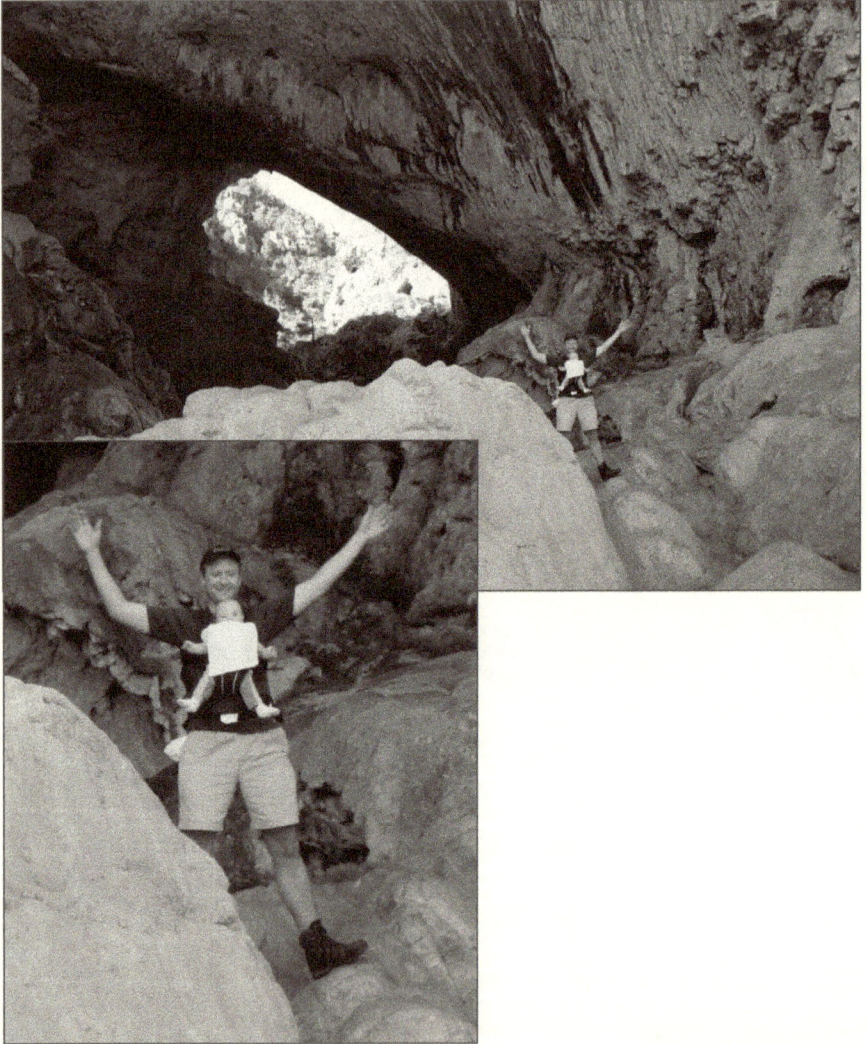

Posted in pics

Oak Creek Canyon Overlook

Posted on September 12, 2012

Look at that…a little family photo! That means someotherbody was working the camera for a change. How handy. Note the beeb has just spotted a yeti and is facing the wrong way. I would be mad at her, but I know very well that you can't stay mad at anyone wearing stripey pants.

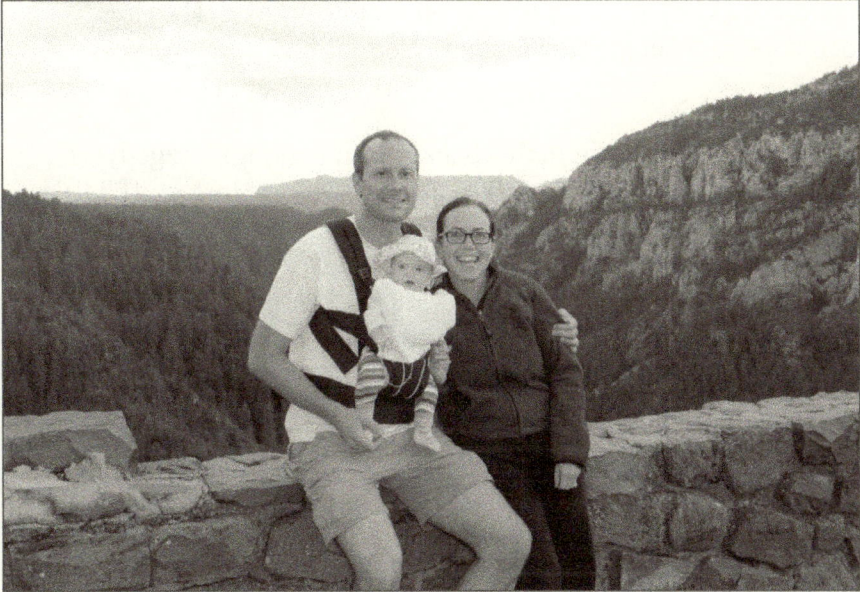

Posted in pics | 1 Reply

Ain't you glad you stayed?

- Grandma A

The beeb's thoughts in the car, as approximated based on observation

Posted on September 13, 2012

La la la la la…..I do love this gentle jostling and the abundance of white noise. Wish I wasn't in this stupid bucket, but at least I have my plastic keys to play with. Mmmmmm…..keys. They're delicious and fun to rattle around. Yep, I loves me some keys…

(drops keys)

Aaaaaaaarrrgggh! I'm in this bucket with nothing! Tragedy! I can't live in a world without keys! How will I unlock stuff?! It's not worth going on any longer! Cruel and evil world!

(Mom hands the keys back)

Hey, look….keys! Man, oh man, that's great. I like keys. Let's see how much I can drool on 'em before the next exit…

Posted in Uncategorized

Thousand yard stare

Posted on September 14, 2012

There's a depth to that stare. I think we've commented on it before. Just somehow shows the eyes of someone much older. Maybe it's not her first time around this world. I'm not going to cut her soul in half and count the rings, but I am going to speculate…

Posted in pics

Sick as a dog

Posted on September 15, 2012

Poor Lily is sick. Her first cold. It's no fun for anyone, although other than sleeping all the time you wouldn't know it from her actions or demeanor. No question she's stuffy and has a chest cough…you can hear it clearly. We're torturing her with saline nose spray, which has two effects: 1) it reeeeaaaaally pisses her off and she goes ballistic, and 2) it loosens up the mucous in her head, and it (the mucous) pours out in a disgusting aftermath. She seems to be feeling OK now – just as laughy and giggly as ever when she's awake. Only wish she could be awake a little more.

Posted in Uncategorized

New game: A Fistful of Dadomite

Posted on September 15, 2012

With the beeb sick and mom and dad struggling to catch up on their sleep, mom has taken to bringing lil' Lily to our bed in the morning. I think you're not supposed to do that, but I support it…it's cute, and it allows us to keep an eye on her while grabbing that last little sliver of important sleep. So the three of us doze in and out and it's a lovely little scene. Some bad news: when she's not asleep herself, the beeb needs entertainment. She has evidently invented a game to play when I'm sleeping and she's not. Here's how it goes: she grabs a handful of my chest hair and attempts to separate it from my skin. Fun for her, sleep disruptive for me. But what are you gonna do, right? Smack her hand? Tell her to stop? She's only entertaining herself and learning about the world around her. Am I gonna deny that to my bebus just because chest hairs are wired directly into the 'maximum pain' portion of the brain and it makes my eyes water? Nope. Not this guy. Tough it out, dad. Man up and take your medicine.

It's not always so bad, by the way. Today she mixed it up and did a new version where she sticks her thumb in my mouth and grabs me like a catfish. Less painful, more weird, equally awakening.

Posted in Uncategorized

C-c-c-c-cat fight

Posted on September 16, 2012

Auntie Bex vs. the Beeb. In this sequence you can see how it developed. All ends well.

First, Lily throws a right cross. Becky bobs her head left and fixes the beeb with a steely glare.

Next, Bex goes to bite Lily in the nose. Lily turns her head and offers her throwaway ear instead. Ears don't taste good, so Bex is deterred.

Finally, they reconcile and share a laugh over how silly it was to be fighting in the first place. I don't think they remember what it was all about anyway. I call it a draw.

She eats like a bird

Posted on September 17, 2012

Check it out…a small but important step…Little Lily now recognizes the bottle and lets you know if she wants it or not. She doesn't exactly order from a menu, mind – she'll either open her mouth and turn toward the bottle or she won't. I call that communication, albeit on a very rudimentary level. If she doesn't do the hungry thing and you still try to feed her, you get the lolling cow tongue and a lot of formula dribbling out all over the place.

Now, I don't think it's very likely…but there's an outside chance that this is learned behavior. Steve and Dena and their beeb Andi were here over the weekend. Andi is great at not only indicating she's hungry, but removing her pacifier and making ready for the feed. Very impressive! Did the bebus witness this and take a page from that very advanced book?! No way to tell of course. We're happy either way. Saves a lot of time, aggravation, and formula when she tells you whether or not to bother.

Posted in pics

Tender moment at the Grand Canyon

Posted on September 18, 2012

Ya gots to feed tha Beeb if you plan on keeping her happy at elevation. You can see here that I'm using my special polarized sunglasses to closely monitor the contents of the bottle (effective despite any potential glare). Lily for her part is dozing & working that bottle again. As she so often does.

Posted in pics

Seeing eye to eye in the old west

Posted on September 19, 2012

So yeah, we went to the Grand Canyon today with grandma and grandpa. It was a great time…we took the train from Williams, AZ to the south rim. Advantage train: minimizes time in the car and therefore (if you're Lily) time in the bucket. When she's in the bucket, she has 2 settings: Off (sleeping) and Pissed (not sleeping). Neither of those is great.

But on the train, boy oh boy!…she was once again the belle of the ball. Our lovely tour guide/local expert Morgan took a shine to her and darn near integrated her into the narrative. They got along famously. I wish we would have thought to get a picture of them.

We DID get a picture of G & G & Beeb. What a great shot, if I may heap praise on the photographer (who happens to be my wife). Everybody looking good, smiling, and enjoying the trip. What could be better than that?

Posted in Meet the bebe

150

Trouble brewing

Posted on September 20, 2012

There's mischief behind that look, I'm sure of it. I can't read her little face except to know her thoughts have strayed beyond doing good & avoiding evil like I told her. She looks like she just decided who's porch gets the flaming bag of poo tonight. I hope it's not mine. I'm tired of stamping them out.

Posted in pics

Aqvabeeb

Posted on September 21, 2012

Not sure why she needs special distilled water, but there you go…you learn stuff while parenting I suppose. My water comes from the tap or the spring or the filtering plant or something. Beebwater is distilled by the elves of evaporation from the tears of unicorns and steeped in the pots of pourri. That's the good stuff, and I'd accept nothing less for her beebness. 79 cents a gallon I'm ponying up for it. No expense spared. Four ounces of that and two scoops of plump juicy formula…it's the simple things in life.

Posted in Uncategorized | 1 Reply

Wow, Lily is fancy. Owen got tap water + formula. We didn't heat it either. I guess he was neglected. ☺

- Erin

A blanket's a blanket of course of course

Posted on September 22, 2012

Aaaaaah, lazy day, and we had a blast....guess who was ticklish? She's not normally but today she was reacting and giggled and laughed herself silly. In fact, her beebness spent a good 45 minutes in the little gym thing rotating from toy to toy and expressing her pleasure with each. Today's big winner aside from the ticklemonster: Pickles The Horse Blanket. Pickles has several key features including a high degree of spit absorption, a washing machine friendly design, and a second use as an actual blanket. The first feature was utilized heavily as always. You can't really let her play with Pickles much without enduring several Godfather jokes, but it's well worth it. Thank you, strange disembodied horse head!

Posted in pics

Because that's how I like to sleep at the table, OK?

Posted on September 23, 2012

Dinner at Elote tonight, courtesy of the visiting troubadours from DC. A thousand thanks to you all! Lily was in rare form, enjoying the population density in the line while we waited and then treating herself to a nap at the table. She also displayed a new technique: sleeping while holding one's own foot. Why she chose to develop and put into use this skill I'll never know. It's pretty sweet though, I must admit. Below you can see for yourself her supercool nap pose....first head on, then in profile, and lastly as a backdrop to the appetizers.

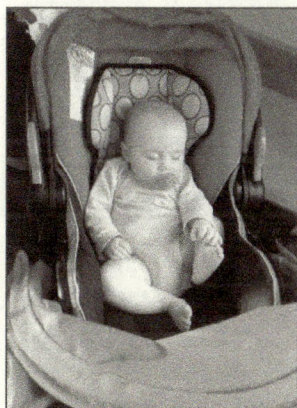

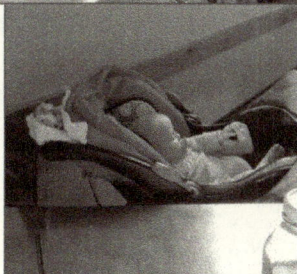

Next time I sleep at dinner I'm doing it for sure. Look out, Thanksgiving attendees!

Posted in pics

Silly hat contest

Posted on September 24, 2012

It's no contest. Winners: those who view this picture.

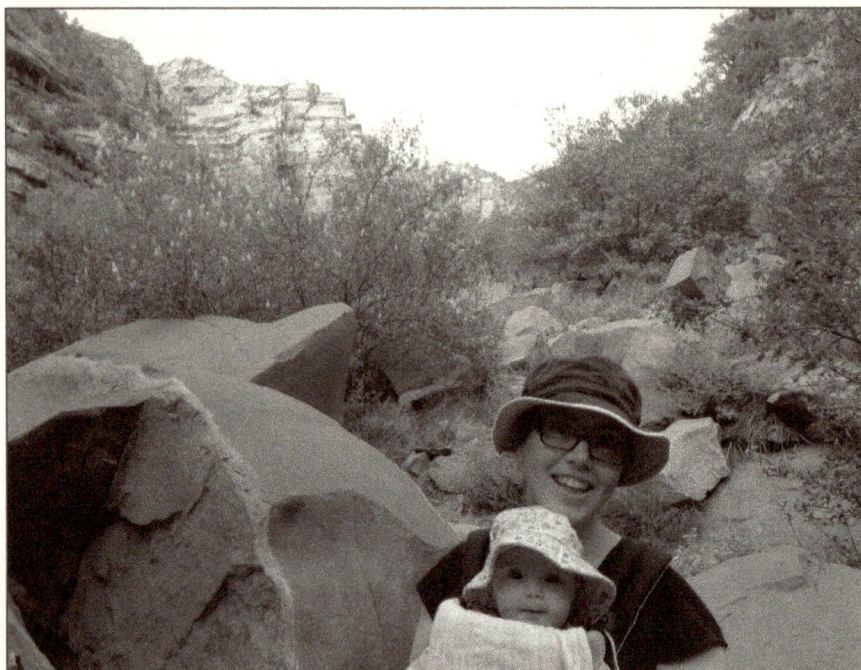

Cute as heck though, right?! Lily too! This was near the end of a little hike we took yesterday or the day before. A nice path marked by Alligator Juniper and Pinion Pine. There was a natural arch but it required a scramble for up-close viewing and the Beeb's not scramble friendly yet. That sounds like it's a pending endorsement for Denny's or the Waffle House or something but it's not meant to be.

Posted in pics

Mouthful of something

Posted on September 25, 2012

Not sure if she's teething or her venom glands have kicked into high gear, but we thought we'd try giving Lily a frozen ring of goo. It went....uh....confusingly. She wasn't convinced that it was something she liked or hated. I can tell you that this initial quizzical look was replaced by one a little more pointed.

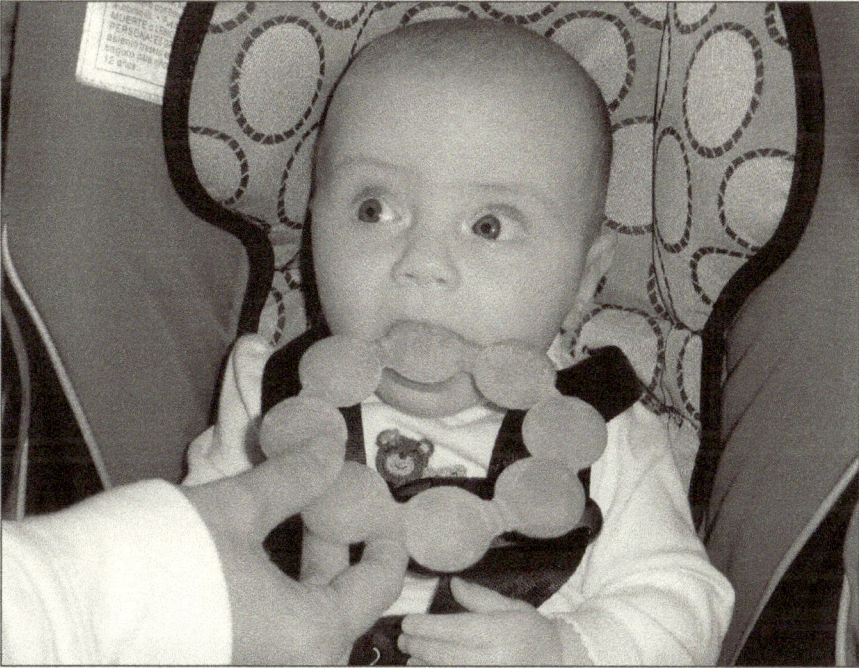

Posted in pics

Less rock, more roll

Posted on September 26, 2012

Ladies and gentlemen, we have a roller on our hands. Back to front on the play mat, then after realizing how much she hates being on her belly......front to back again. We're gonna need a bigger play mat. Squeaking and babbling the whole time as you would expect. I guess rocking will come when she's able to sit up more proficiently. She's doing that just a little bit so far...not enough to earn a merit badge or anything. Soon as she nails it, we'll have rock & roll with a side of babble & squeak. Another page stolen from the English playbook!

Posted in Uncategorized

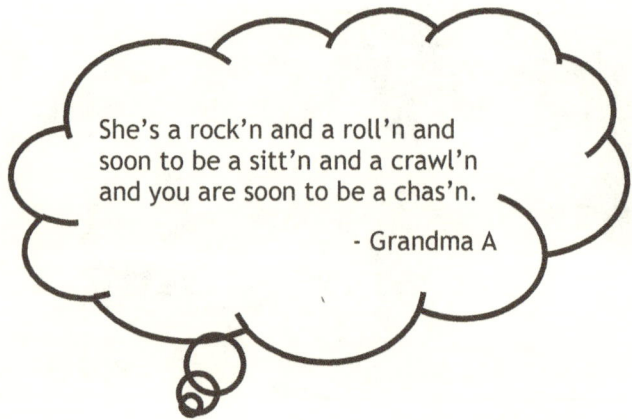

She's a rock'n and a roll'n and soon to be a sitt'n and a crawl'n and you are soon to be a chas'n.

- Grandma A

She hates these ears!

Posted on September 27, 2012

Trying to pull them off for reasons unknown. Our theory is simple: she found 'em. Just exploring her little bebus body parts. That's much preferred to the other explanation, which would be an ear infection or other medical complication. This is one instance where we're hoping our little daughter fails…if she were to succeed at removing the beebears, it would mean a lifetime without sunglasses and earrings. Tough call.

Posted in Uncategorized | 1 Reply

Uhhhh…..beeb….you're doing it wrong again….

Posted on September 28, 2012

Lovely Lily is capable now of handling her own pacifier. Grab it, twirl it around, and back in the ol' gob without much interference from us larger types. I totally dig it. It would be too much to expect her to get it right from the get-go….and sure enough she's doing things her own way – grabbing the pacifier by the nipple and chewing on the edge. Whatever, right?! It's all made from the same material. Who cares, as long as she's delivering it to the mouth and chewing happily in a way that keeps her occupied. So mission accomplished! But from a purist's perspective, uh…beeb….you're doing it wrong.

Posted in pics

159

Transition back home: not very smooth

Posted on September 29, 2012

Oooooooooh, man. It's a long day of travel from Sedona to New York, even for an adult. We thought it was going OK – Lily was kind enough to sleep in the car from Sedona to Phoenix, then again on the way to the airport. But she wore down over the course of the day. We had a bumpy flight (literally, I mean…turbulence) and we were pummeled with beebtears more than once. Then in the car on the way back into the city she completely lost her mind. We got 20 solid minutes of full-bore pissed off hatecrying. Generous folks that we are, we shared it with our zen master cab driver. He must have a bushel of kids & grandkids because he didn't raise an eyebrow. Good man. Beeb gets all sweaty when she cries like that, by the way. It's quite a workout I guess. Anyway when we finally got to the apartment and picked her up, she burped…and then was all smiles again. Go figure.

The time differential is still working against us now that we're back east. And I'm afraid we weren't terribly diligent with her sleep schedule while we were away. In short: we're in for some long nights this week. Let us know if you need a random wake-up call between 2 and 5 am. Happy to oblige.

Posted in Uncategorized

Wrong role model

Posted on September 30, 2012

Continuing her voyage of self-discovery, Lily is now happily pulling at her little feet (which is terribly cute!) and grabbing her girl junk (which is not). Great. Too many Madonna videos I suspect. Thank goodness she's still too young for this to require a conversation to make her stop. Hoping she grows out of it before she starts attending birthday parties and stuff…

Posted in Uncategorized

October

Beeb down, and looking plumper

Posted on October 1, 2012

Well, that's one way to sleep I guess. Not sure I've ever chosen that pose myself, but to each her own. I also don't normally sleep holding my foot…

Check out that gut, by the way. I think maybe she started eating surreptitious nachos after we fall asleep or something. Better not be hitting my private nacho stash or we'll be having terse words. Keep outta my nachos, bebus.

Posted in pics

New nanny, new wardrobe choices

Posted on October 2, 2012

Starting at nanny: Natalie. Miss Natalie seems very calm, very soothing, and very knowledgeable about how to deal with a bebus. Good news for us, and I include Lily in that. The new regimen includes calisthenics in the morning…not a joke…a series of stretches to promote a healthier, more limber child I suppose. I'm not going to push back on physical therapy. I think it's good. It also helps to explain the wardrobe choice we faced when we got home the other night. The photo's blurry, I know…sorry. Regardless, you can clearly see Lily was dressed in gray sweatpants & wifebeater t-shirt. She even has a little gut hanging out again. Supersweet. I suspect she was working a side of beef like a heavy bag somewhere in the Bronx (crackin' da ribs), then she ran up some stairs two at a time, threw her hands aloft and choked out a triumphant but garbled message of proclamation. I'm getting her a little knit hat for the winter.

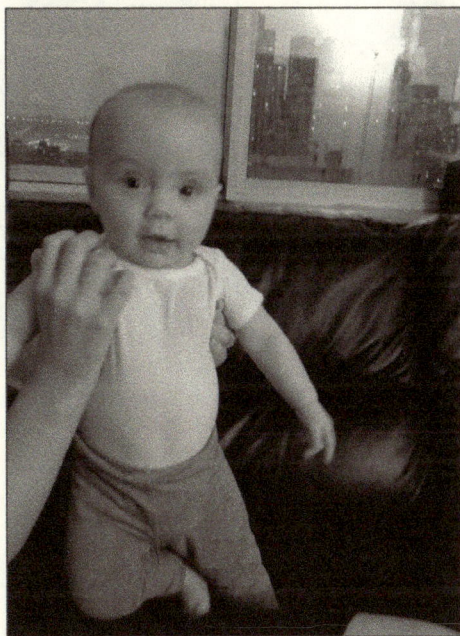

Mr. Dan, long overdue!

Posted on October 3, 2012

Now how the heck did I miss this one? Good pic of Dan and the beeb from up in Maine…but that was a long time ago now. Not sure what happened. No matter.

Poor Lily looks a little overwhelmed by the situation, eyes popped open and slightly askew. Back when she was young, remember?!

Posted in Flashback, Meet the bebe

Made for walkin'…and ponies.

Posted on October 4, 2012

Too good to be true! We've been thrilled to receive a generous pile of leftover clothes from a host of friends and relatives. It's soooo nice…no need for us to refresh the wardrobe, it just takes care of itself. If they hadn't sent it over gratis, I'd be looking for a place where I could buy baby clothes by the pound. Long as they're within a suitable size range and somewhere north of disgusting on the hygiene-o-meter, I'd be all over that stuff.

Back to the point: Kathy and Gramma A spent a good deal of time packaging up all the duds. Grouped by size, season, and likely some other characteristics that my fashion-challenged brain couldn't possibly comprehend. With a growing bebus and a change of seasons, we've been rifling some of the boxes to see what all's in there. And what did we discover the other day? Pink glitter boots, amigo. The real deal. Best footwear I've seen since that weird pony-in-the-box chucked a demonic glitter hoof onto my dinner table.

Surely if Lily were to wear the boots, she could coax the pony out of the box, right? And if it came out, she could ride it…. And if she rode it, I can only believe that 3 other pink ponies would shortly follow. The 4 ponygirls of the Pinkpocalypse. I shudder to think.

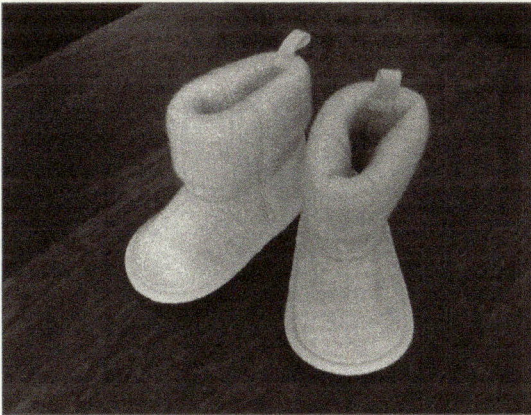

Posted in pics

Son, you got a pie crust on your head

Posted on October 5, 2012

Still battling a little cradle cap. That means a big crusty place on the front of her head. Gross but harmless. Tastes horrible.* Doc said to work it with olive oil and over time it'll go away. OK, them's the orders. Meanwhile she's got a modified Gorbachev look going....I should dye it for halloween maybe.

*No, I didn't eat it. What's wrong with you?!

Posted in Uncategorized

Piper down again

Posted on October 6, 2012

Miss Natalie brought the beeb to see mom at work today. Here she is looking pretty well tuckered out. Notables:
- Ladybug continues to be a featured toy, one of our go-to's
- No matter what toys you offer, the plain white burp cloth winds up in her hands more often than not
- First time in jeans (well, stretchy jeans anyway)
- How 'bout them chipmunk cheeks?!

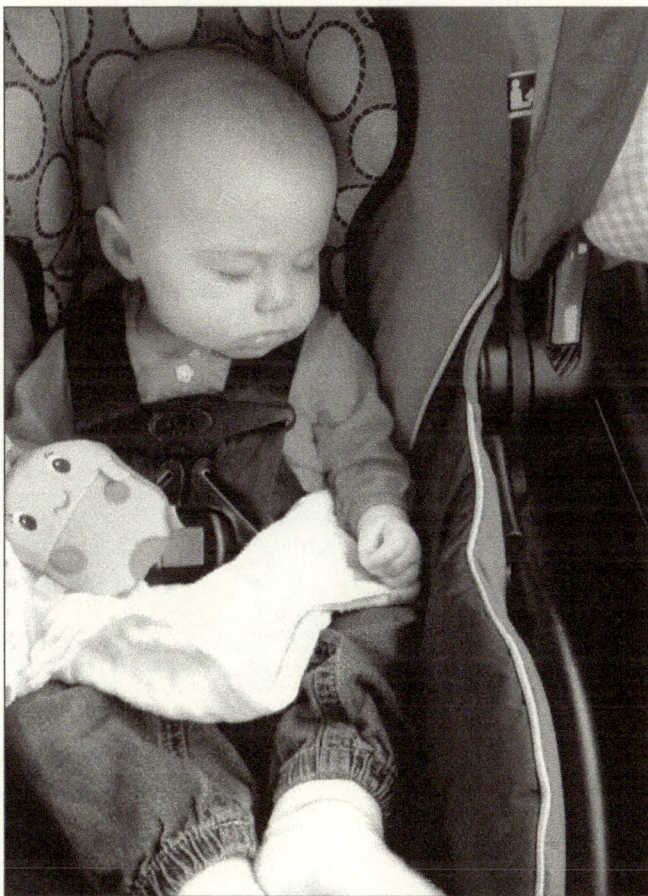

Posted in pics

168

Just standin' in the creek

Posted on October 7, 2012

Here we are in Oak Creek north of Sedona. It's Grasshopper Point, named long ago for the freakishly large and abundant bugs. We saw one of them and I gotta say I was impressed. Looked like it could take off a finger if it wanted to. We steered clear. Lily was pretty well fascinated by the noise and visual show provided by the water rushing over some rocks. We stood ankle deep and enjoyed it. That's the whole story. Wish there was more action or whatever, but that would likely mean I fell in. Lame.

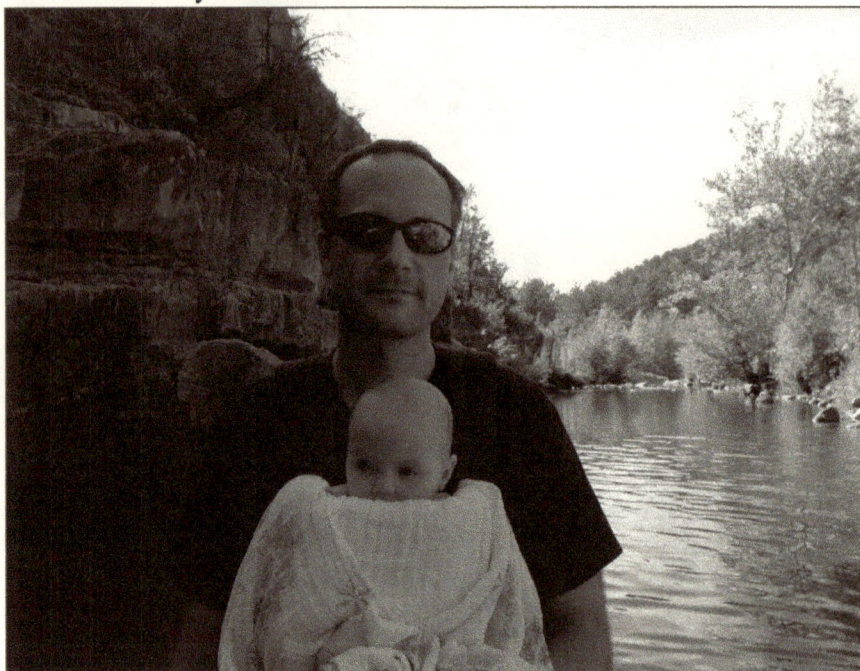

Posted in pics

2-2?!

Posted on October 8, 2012

What's that, slankethead? Yeah, a quarter of the way through the season already and it's more of the same…injuries and losses to teams you should have beaten. Hmmmm? You think so? You're probably right. And yeah – 31 points and you still can't win? I hear ya – something's wrong. But – how's that? Um hmm… His knee still isn't right but he looked OK, didn't he? That's helping Timmons as well of course. But I don't see the beard anywhere….the D line just isn't dominating the way you expect. I think they're OK though, don't you? I mean – if they can go 3-1, 3-1, and 3-1 in the next quarters they're fine. Oooh, you think so, eh? Don't worry my mind, slankethead. There's a lot of season left!

Posted in pics

Plenty of formula embiggens the smallest bebe

Posted on October 9, 2012

13lbs 4oz at the 6-month checkup today. Not too bad, Miss Lily! She continues her slow climb up the percentiles…now 5th-6th percentile vs. full term babies and 13th-15th vs. preemies (depending on the category). Know what that means?….she's inside two standard deviations on the full term curve! Her highest percentile is head diameter, by the way, which prompted me to call her 'Charlie Brown' for the duration of the visit. I don't think her tender feelings were damaged by that. They were damaged by the 3 shots she got in the thigh. She toughed it out.

Posted in Uncategorized

Grueling day

Posted on October 10, 2012

The beeb got her first taste of 'real food' today after we got back from Boston. Truthfully, it's the farthest thing in the world from real food. It's gruel. I mean the stuff they'd feed you in a damp and windowless cell in some faraway land, where the only shot you have at reemergence is that Rambo himself needs to free someone you're with. Here's the recipe for those of you wanting to try it at home: 4 parts formula, 1 part powdered organic whole oats. Mmmmmmmm! You see it on every menu these days. At least in the nice parts of town. Normally garnished with ramps, but we skipped that. Check out the photo montage:

Preparing for the big event. Looking spooked? A little nervous? She can't tell us whether or not she had butterflies.

First tentative bites from Mom. Trusting now. Feeling it out…

Finding the rhythm. Starting to take over and run the show!

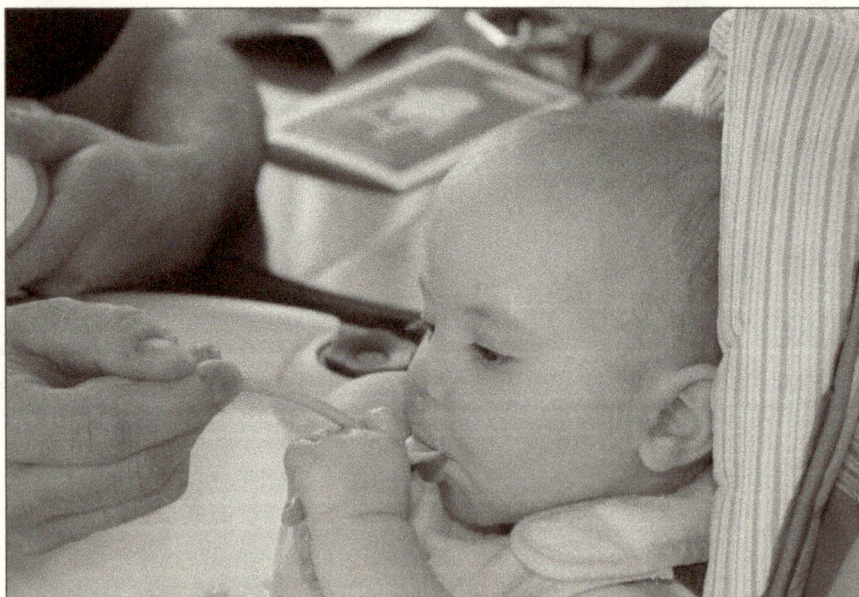

Mom and Dad no longer in sight. Spoon in mouth, on a solo mission.

Old hat.

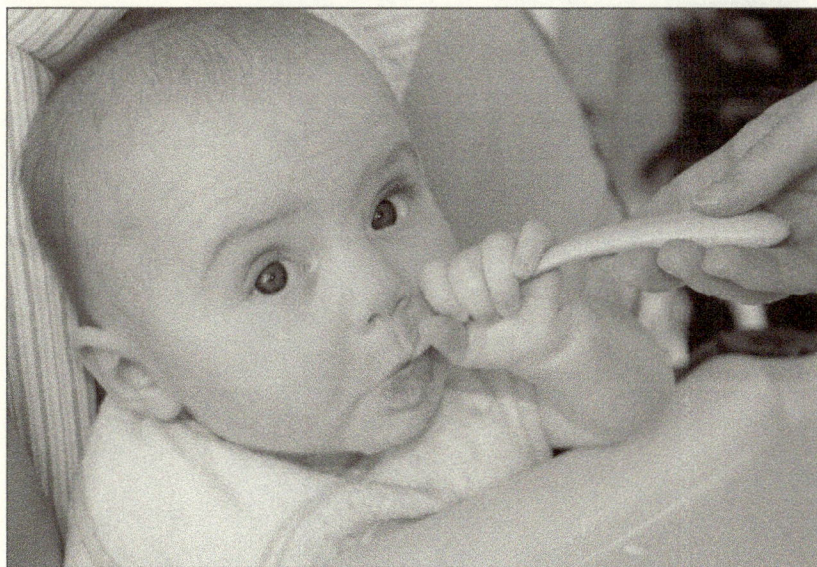

All in the span of an hour. Go beeb, and welcome to the Thanksgiving table!

Posted in pics

Lily Ray Charles

Posted on October 11, 2012

Not good enough to sing and play simultaneously, but you can see she's vocalizing here. Just prior, she was bashing at the keyboard. I mean bashing! A little more Jerry Lee Lewis than Ray Charles, come to think of it. Light on the finesse and heavy on the attitude! Not tall enough to throw a foot up there although I assume that will come in good time.

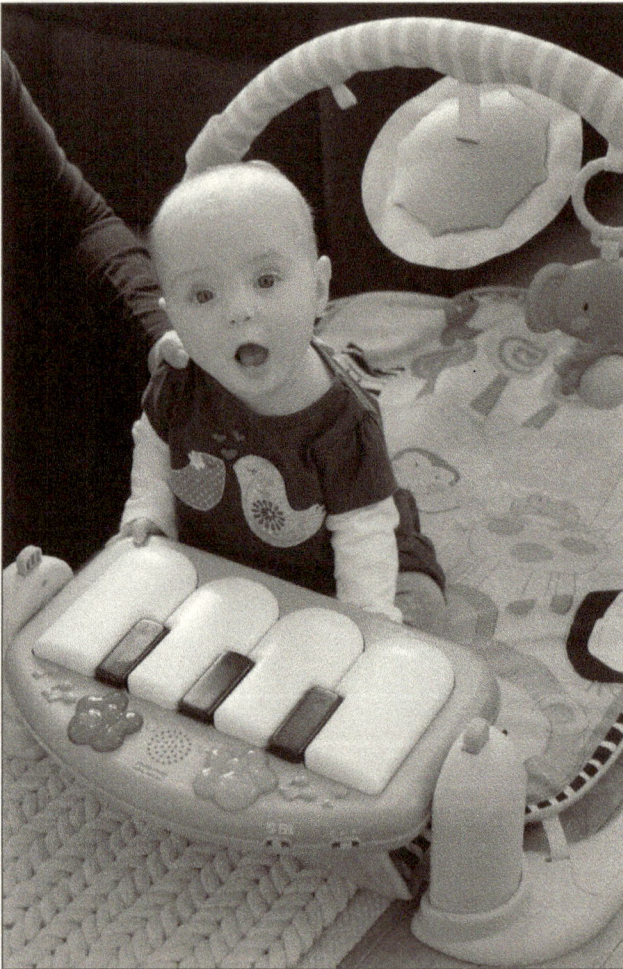

Posted in pics

It's alive!

Posted on October 12, 2012

No, Lily. It just spins and the little balls inside it rattle around and stuff. Sorry to disappoint. She does look a bit like a mad scientist in there though, right?! There's a lot going on and she's overwhelmed by each little component in the jumper thing. It's a recipe for sensory overload (which, by the way, we achieved tonight when dad got home all excited and came at her like a spider monkey). Fear not beebophiles, I won't let her create new life or otherwise engage in madly scientific activities until she grows appropriately crazy hair and starts wearing her goggles like I told her.

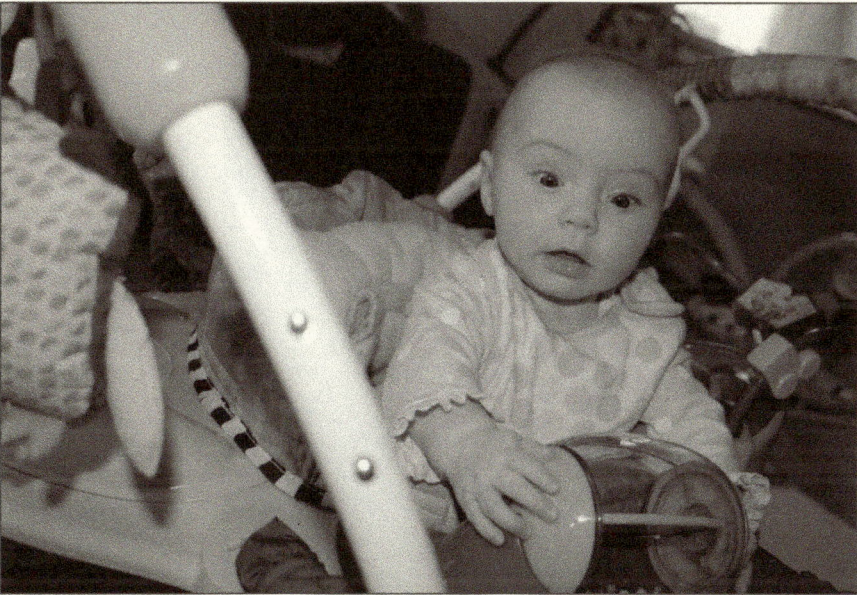

Posted in pics

Benjamin Button

Posted on October 13, 2012

Check out Lily masquerading as a little old man. This was many months ago. She was all skinny and old. With that grumpy face, I'd bet she's pissed about those whipper snapper kids throwing a frisbee on the lawn again (dag nabbit!).

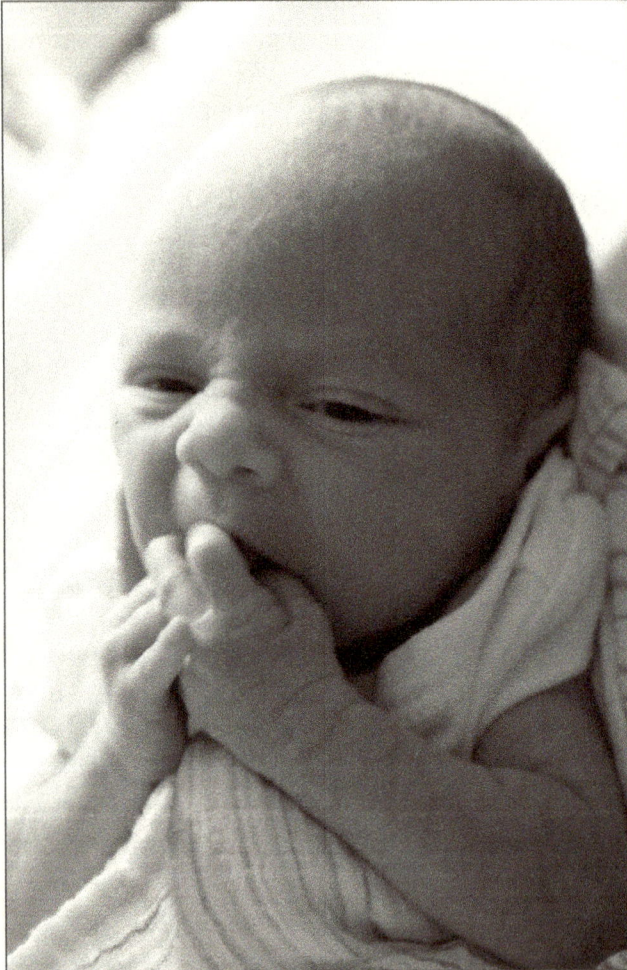

Posted in Flashback, pics

Play dates are ON

Posted on October 15, 2012

Miss Natalie is plugging into the social scene here, and I'm pretty sure little Lily will have more friends than us in short order. She might have been caught off guard for the photo – she's making a face like she is a) crapping her pants again, or b) stealing something. Maybe she heisted a toy…that would explain why looked me dead in the eye tonight and said, "Daddy, how do you find a fence that won't snitch?*".

* Language skills still not perfected, so it sounded like a growl or grunt or some such thing. But I knew what she meant.

Now yawning in Technicolor!

Posted on October 16, 2012

Yeah, I know we already discussed the eating thing so it's not news. But it's fun for the whole family! We're going to work through this by color, which is evidently what you do. Up today: orange. Not oranges…heard bad things about citrus…nope, first up is carrots. So she had some carrots today. It went about as smoothly as it did with the gruel, with the exception of an initial stink face. High comedy! Here are some stills, then a link to the video. We're at rOy g biv. 1 down, 6 to go!

Eating forlornly:

Eating confusedly:

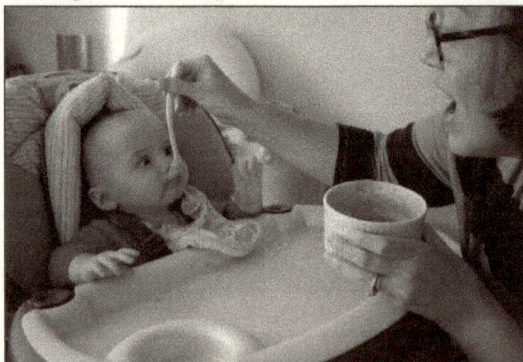

Posted in pics, Videos

Tired

Posted on October 17, 2012

Man, that girl is tired at the end of the day lately. It's all we can do to keep her awake through bath time and then a bottle. I don't know if it's because she's having such full days, or if it's the new food, or what. She's bushed though. (Speaking of the dietary changes and with my apologies once again for the toilet comments…3 poops today…maybe that's sapping her energy.) Anyway, girl needs to eat. We'll need to find a way to navigate that and keep her fattening!

Posted in Uncategorized

Public display of furniture use

Posted on October 18, 2012

That's right….the high chair is in play! We've used it twice now –
once at a dim sum place in Brooklyn (after visiting Christine, Erin
and their little brood) and once at local favorite french pastry place /
strategic butter reserve La Bergamote. Pic below is from the dim
sum place. Who's a happy girlie in the chair? The beeb, that's who.

Posted in pics

181

Daddy time

Posted on October 19, 2012

This is embarrassing, but what the hey. Evidently the approved technique for playing with Lily is comprised of equal parts of the following:
- Making idiot faces
- Pretending to eat her extremities
- Growling while gnawing on her stomach and neck
- Mixing in a quick game of "In your grill"
- Poking at her in a mocking way

We're spending a heck of a lot of time on the floor these days. Might seem normal for the little 'un, but it's a voyage of rediscovery for me. It was enough to inspire us to find a new housekeeper…we can't soak up all the grime with our clothes, you know.

Posted in Videos

Pile o' rings

Posted on October 20, 2012

Looks like the beeb is concentrating here, eh? She doesn't really grasp the concepts this toy is meant to teach, but she did demonstrate her willingness to eat bright orange plastic donuts.

Posted in pics

Upon further review

Posted on October 21, 2012

OK, we've just reviewed a 13 minute video taken today of Lily's play-date with little Mia from downstairs. It's horribly cute. Mia's a sweetheart, very good natured, all smiles. She's significantly larger than the beeb but that's to be expected (what with our spawn's weeness, as previously discussed). Here's what we learned…

- The beeb needs work on her sharing. She spent an awful lot of time trying to grab Mia's crinkle square. It didn't matter how many times Miss Natalie took it away, gave it back to Mia, and told Lily to play with her own toys…the beeb just tried to thieve it again. Note to parents: teach your kid how to share. Clearly we have not done this.

- The beeb still puts everything in her mouth. Everything. If you were to give her a hornets nest dipped in super glue and rolled in broken glass, she'd try to stuff it in her mouth. I'm hoping it's just the shark thing…she's testing and learning and that requires all 5 senses to be engaged. Other possible explanations include: she's starving and desperately trying to eat, she's related to pac man, and she's preparing for a fight by strengthening her jaw muscles.

- The beeb can straight *sit*. It's taken her a while to get it, but now it looks like the only two things that can throw her off her sit are 1) boredom, and 2) reaching too far for some other kid's toy, which she would of course stuff in her mouth.

- The beeb likes hanging out with other beebs. They yapped at each other a little. There was some squealing and some flailing of limbs. There were several near head-butts, but nothing intentional. I think they really enjoyed each other's company.

Nice work, Miss Natalie. Good comedy today.

Posted in Uncategorized

New game: George Washington

Posted on October 23, 2012

Lily's favorite toy of all is the burp cloth. Simple, unassuming, and ubiquitous. And now it's the centerpiece of the new game "George Washington". Here's how it goes… you fold the burp cloth, toss it across her head, and then call her George Washington a bunch while attempting to hold a conversation. It's very similar to the old staple 'slankethead', but with a more noble and historic feel.

Posted in pics

185

De-eating

Posted on October 25, 2012

Lily's big on de-eating. She has two primary methods, both of which will be familiar to you. There is less good news with the oral variant…just means she's barfing on us again. Now that she's started solid foods (in the 'orange' spectrum), her other de-eating has taken a turn for the worse. Well, not worse…it's taken a turn for the different. No more runny diaper blow-outs – hooray! Now we get proper poops. Boo! Time to hook up a diaper genie or some such thing before our current diaper disposal solution gets overwhelmed.

Posted in Uncategorized

Feed the beeb

Posted on October 26, 2012

We're at rOy G biv as of yesterday. Green is the new orange, dietarily speaking. The beeb sucked down a bowl of peas like she'd done it a thousand times before. Mr. Andrew was in the house lending a hand and he came away virtually unscathed (a failed attempt with a sippy-cup of water left his jeans damp but not his spirit....he knew the first three rows were designated splash areas and he chose not to wear his poncho).

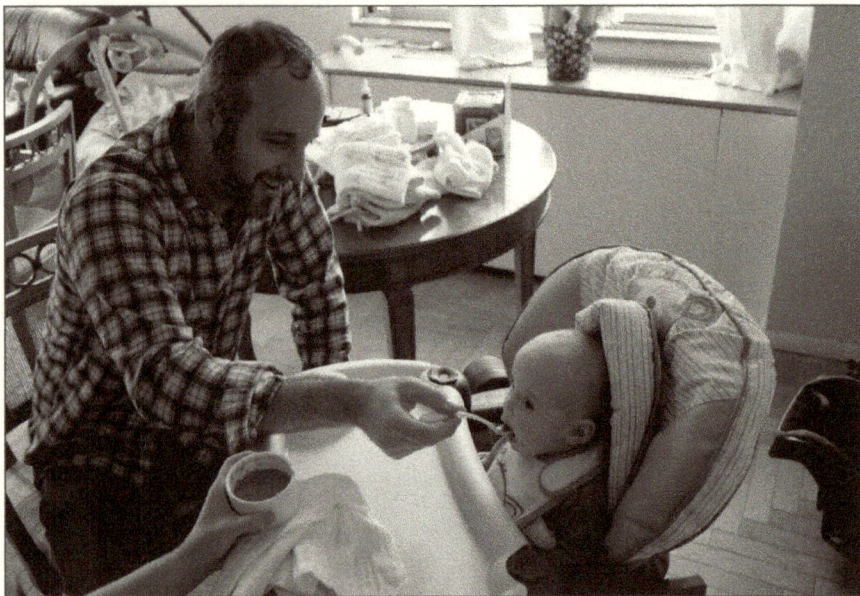

Posted in Meet the bebe, pics | 2 Replies

BEARD????? I like it.

    - Grandpa A

I like beards, too. I should grow one!

    - Editor

Piano lessons continued

Posted on October 27, 2012

Check her out: part pianist, part hummingbird. Her hands are moving so fast that they're just a blur! You can imagine the dominant rendition of 'chopsticks' that is coming so very soon…

Posted in pics | 1 Reply

I've been taking piano lessons for ten years and I can't do that!!!!

- Grandpa A

And that's why you wipe the table down

Posted on October 28, 2012

Lily is enjoying the high chair these days, probably because it puts her at the correct height for table consumption. I don't mean eating at the table. I mean eating the table. Demonstrated below.

Apologies for the grainy photo – evidently the camera was more interested in the dude photobombing me in the background there (who appears to be using sign language to order a footlong hot dog).

Posted in pics

189

Squash soup and tzatziki

Posted on October 29, 2012

Two quick moments from the day I'd like to share:
1. Bebe made squash soup tonight. How, you ask? She waited until she was in her little bath tub (which holds maybe 3 gallons of water and rests within our larger adult-sized tub) and then she barfed squash everywhere. Very gross. Medium chunky. Forced a draining & refilling of said tub for a proper cleaning.
2. Mom was holding the beeb, and she (mom) walked into the kitchen to test some tzatziki I was making. I held out a spoonful to her and Lily naively opened up her little mouth like she would do the tasting. Very cute. Wish I got a photo of that.

Posted in Uncategorized

It was a good and victorious nap

Posted on October 30, 2012

Mom and the Bebe took an adorable nap today. Mom eventually got up (before I could photograph them both) and snapped this shot. Lily's in a pose that is consistent with the message on the bib, but really she should be awake and stage-diving. Exact same pose, just with open eyes and a different backdrop. Maybe I should do a little photo editing? I can grab some open eyes off of a public domain pic…maybe yellow…maybe red….dunno….gotta think about that.

Luckily, this pic also summarizes our experience with Hurricane Sandy. Made a mess of New York but not of our apartment. Luck shone upon us.

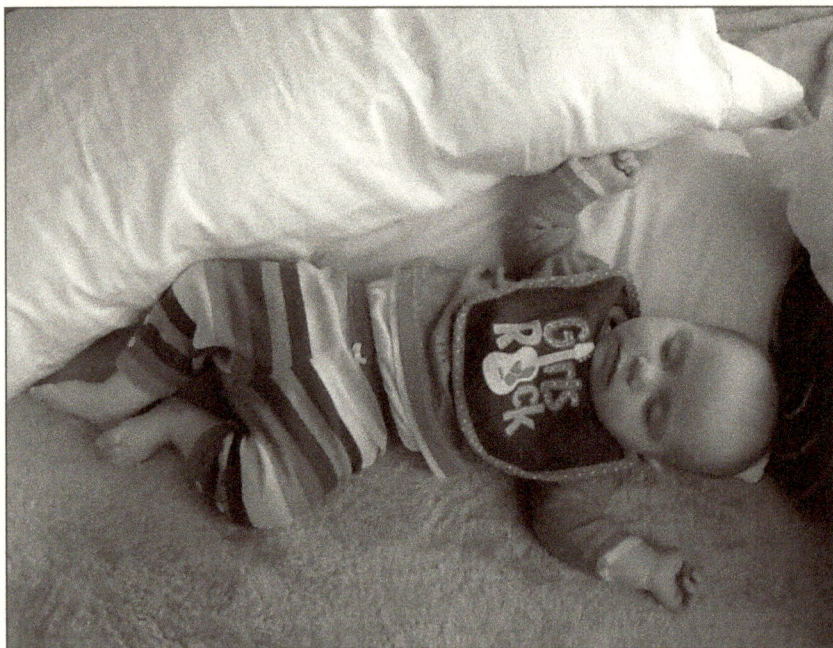

Posted in pics

191

November

High maintenance

Posted on November 1, 2012

Well, miss Lily is quickly developing in a very unfortunate area: she's becoming high maintenance. Example: she'll play happily on the floor by herself for a good long while…unless you leave the room. You leave and she immediately starts this strange mongrel cry / scream / whine noise using her 'outside' volume. No good. She gave mom a good dose of the same last night at bath time. Why, you ask? Mom had the audacity to take away the little scooper thing we use to pour water on her. Never mind that the beeb was surrounded by no fewer than 4 floaty bath toys. She wanted the scooper, dammit. And taking it away was not to her liking. Cryscreamwhine!!

We're going to ride this one out for a little while to see if she outgrows it. If not, Lord help us, we're going to have to try to break her like a wild horse. If I was a bettin' man, I'd bet against us.

Posted in Uncategorized

193

Tickling the ivories again

Posted on November 2, 2012

The beeb on the piano once more! In this performance, she actually bashes successfully at the keys for a second or two! Aaaaaah, yeah. You'll notice the phone sitting nearby, just begging for an agent to call. You'll also notice that our interest in the piano is pretty short-lived. It ended with an attempt to eat the keyboard. That attempt was not successful. Her previous effort to destroy the other keyboard with a well-placed barf was.

Slankethead on the Giants

Posted on November 3, 2012

Hey, Slankethead….what do you think about the Steelers oddball travel plans for the Giants game this weekend? Oh yeah? Sure, why not?! I read they were planned to stay in Jersey City, so it's got to be better than that! Ummm hmmm. Yep, yep, I know. Legursky played well for those games though. And the running backs are getting healthier as well. Seems Haley's got the offense going pretty well. What? Ooooh. I suppose so. And, wait – what's that? No idea. You really think that's a possibility? They better I suppose, or it's back to .500 again. We'll see, Slankethead, we'll see!

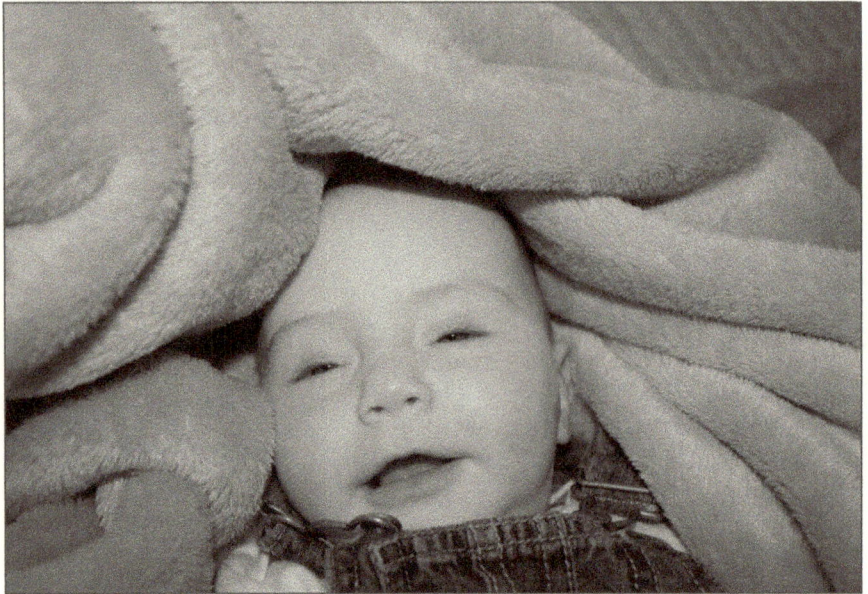

Posted in pics

Fruiting

Posted on November 5, 2012

Applesauce is officially on the menu. Mom made it with red apples and it was delicious. Also threw a banana down the ol' gullet and the beeb dug that as well. We're desperately hoping she keeps eating the way she has been…as a hungry, open minded, and relatively clean little girl. Her gut is growing steadily these days. We've come a long way, bebus! ROY G biv at this point. I suppose we can score some blueberries and a plum, which I'll count as either indigo or violet. Or maybe as both. Not sure my man-eyes can differentiate between the two anyway. Whatever. Keep that mouth open, Lily, and don't start getting picky on us!

Posted in Uncategorized

Election results are in

Posted on November 7, 2012

The clear winner in the Bath-time Companion Election 2012 is....Turtle. Oh, she flirted with Octopus for a long time. He (or she?) is blue and has lots of limbs. Kinda shaped like a pacifier, really. I can see why she'd dig it. Crab was in the race for a while as well – probably due to the bright red coloration. I think the absence of protruding limbs did him in (or her). So Lily puts that damn turtle in her mouth and then talks throughout a 'normal' bath. Poor delicious turtle. Fish? Completely ignored. She couldn't care less about Fish.

Dad prefers Crab because Crab's squirtability is superior to the others. In fact Turtle and Fish don't have the ability to squirt water at all, owing to a manufacturing flaw (the official description of which is 'narrow squirt hole' but don't mention it to them – they're surprisingly sensitive about it).

So there you go. Turtle gets the nod and will serve as Primary Bath-time Companion until he is successfully eaten, impeached, or (most likely) drifts from favor and is displaced by one of the others. Fish is disgraced. Stay away, loser Fish. Nobody likes you. For now.

Posted in pics

Earning her keep

Posted on November 9, 2012

Here's workbeeb, keeping mom company in the office thanks to the shutdown of the NY subway system in the aftermath of Superstorm Sandy. Note the green slanket has found its way into the hallowed halls of Mom's workplace. Also note Lily demonstrating common pacifier protocol these days: hold the nipple and eat the tether. Brilliant.

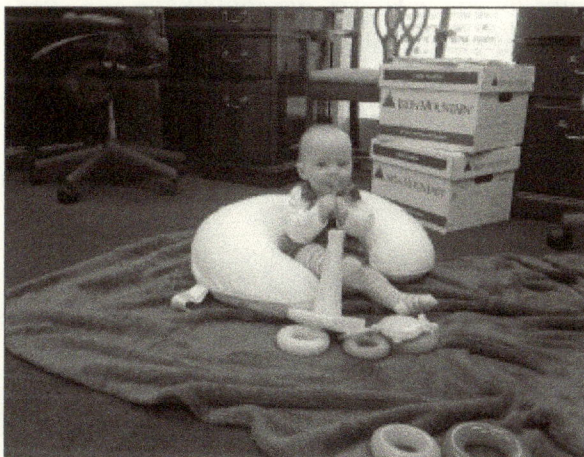

Posted in pics

Frenchy le Havre returns

Posted on November 11, 2012

Tat tat tat…bonjour once again, sweet bebous! I thought it waise to check een on you, for it has beeen some taim since the last we speak-ed. I must say your family of neander-thal parents continues to revolt me. I hear-ed through the grip vine that you travelled today to an aircraft carrier to see the spaece shuttle. One symbol of swain American imperialism sitting atop another, no?! What a wast of taime. Were you were at Chateau le Havre, we could have gone to du Louvre and seen some culture instaid. So sorry, young bebous, that life hates you in zees way. Do not despair, but continue to resist. Your taim will come!

Posted in Uncategorized

Rough day

Posted on November 12, 2012

Not for the beeb, mind…mostly for mom, who got stuck in an all-day meeting and didn't get home until after bedtime. Very sad. Luckily Miss Natalie was able to stay until dad got back somewhat late. No big deal on that front – we did a turbo bath and chucked her straight into the nursery. I think she was asleep before she hit the ground (speaking figuratively here). Unflappable, that one.

Posted in Uncategorized

Oh, that's just GREAT.

Posted on November 13, 2012

So there's a knock on the door tonight, and it's the cops. And I open the door and invite them in....we all take a seat. And they proceed to tell me that Lily has been involved in an incident during a play date. An *incident*? What the heck does that mean?! Well, it means that the beeb got a little riled up with her good friend Mia and attacked her. I wouldn't have believed it, but the cops had photographic evidence and I'm ashamed to admit it's incontrovertible. Here you go, for the record: the Beeb tries to rip Mia's ear off:

Now…we got lucky. Lily is a fraction of Mia's size. Mia is wonderfully mellow. And, gods be praised, her ears are firmly attached. There was really no damage done. Still, guess what you get for a first offense in the Borough of Manhattan? I'll tell you: an hour in solitary. Oh, sure – they give you a ball and you can bum smokes and stuff. But it's a long hour, I hear….just you and your thoughts and your wifebeater and your ball. Here she is, steely eyed and hardened:

They say it changes you. That you can't make it on the outside any more. I hope that's not the case, bebus. Get out of the ear removal game before it's too late. We still believe there's some good in you.

New game demonstrated

Posted on November 14, 2012

Check out mom playing the latest made up game. In this one (which is unnamed), you look all around the beeb and wonder aloud where she might be. Then, suddenly, you make eye contact with her and declare, "There she is!" It's like peekaboo but without the burp cloth. Hiding in plain sight.

We did take it too far once. In our exuberance, we changed "There she is!" into "THERE SHE IS!!" and it scared the hell out of her. Got the water works and a colossal scaredy face. Ooops. Our bad, beeb. Or yours for being a wuss…

Anyway, mom has her going good with a belly laugh and some happy arm gyrations. Then Lily spots the camera and shuts down the fun. Game over, man. Game over.

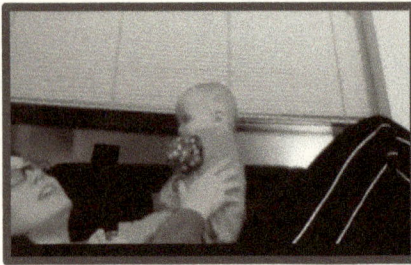

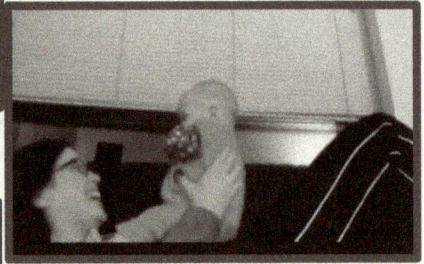

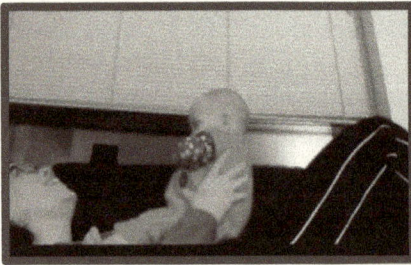

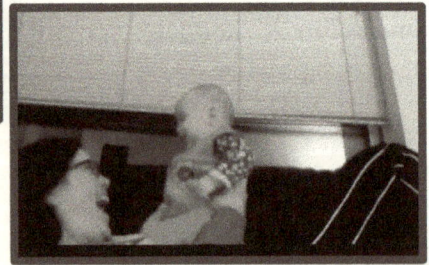

Posted in Videos

She puking up The Hulk?

Posted on November 15, 2012

Going back now to a feeding time of recent yore. You'll never guess what she was eating that day*. Hint: if you look closely around her mouth, there is actually some visible evidence of the meal (really!). There is also evidence that she may retain those blue eyes, although we're led to believe they don't settle down until the first birthday.

* It was radioactive waste. We were hoping for a 'toxic avenger' style mutation that would grant her superhuman powers of some kind but are as yet sorely disappointed.

Posted in pics

Gonna need a rebathing

Posted on November 16, 2012

Once again, it was a matter of time....and today was the day. Lily sh*t the tub. Very sad I wasn't here for the event, which left mom traumatized and unsure about the effectiveness of the bath. I didn't get much in the way of gory details – only that there was a concentrated effort on behalf of the beeb and that there were some precursor bubbles blown. Lowbrow comedy, thou art mine daughter.

Update from this morning
After an additional investigation, it was determined that it was not a Baby Ruth.

Posted in Uncategorized

205

What are we calling her these days?

Posted on November 18, 2012

A couple of new nicknames for the beeb…

First, we're actually using her name quite a bit. That's historically unusual but will no doubt become the norm as soon as she learns to respond to it. For now, it's like calling a cat by their proper name. They just don't care.

Second, she's getting a fair measure of "Cranklepuss". She's a little cranky now and again (as any beeb should be reasonably expected to be), and she'll let you know it. Dripping with attitude.

Third, we're throwing some "Plankton" into the mix. Why Plankton? Because she's planking again, of course. When normal complaining isn't satisfying her, she does a full-body plank and yells at you. Planking no good for getting her into the high chair. Or the stroller. It *is* pretty useful when you're trying to get her little corduroy pants on. Straight legs work well for that.

Posted in Uncategorized

Early morning musings

Posted on November 19, 2012

OK – so this was crazy cute. Lily woke up this morning and spent a little happy time in the crib before demanding we extract her. Here's how it went down: Mom jumped in the shower, but before she did, she put the baby monitor next to me in the bed. In my early morning haze I was drifting in and out for what must have been no more than 10 or 15 minutes. With my open eye, I'm watching the beeb as she lies there. She's on her back, hands clasped, rolling back and forth and going, "Bah. Bah. Bah." Just practicing I suppose. Today's early morning hours were sponsored by the letter B. You can never be sure what's going through her mind when she's doing stuff like that….is she really just mastering the phonetics of B? Is she trying to indicate she wants a bottle? Or that she's a bebus? The conspiracy theorist in me says she was going for 'bowel movement' and purposely ruining my sleep by taunting me about what awaited. And await it did, by the way. From cute to nasty in a heartbeat. There exists no swifter remedy for the malady of 'cute' than a diaper full of turd.

Posted in Uncategorized

207

Advantage: bib

Posted on November 22, 2012

Lily wearing the bib….it's like being at the Red Lobster all-you-can-eat buffet for the entire day. Why, just minutes ago she barfed on herself and guess what? No worries. None for the beeb and none for auntie Bex (who was holding her) either. Exactly what I do at the buffet…barf & carry on undisturbed. How nicely does that tie in with today's plans? Way to point the way beeb!

Posted in Uncategorized

Lily turded on my leg (as she does)

Posted on November 24, 2012

On paper, it's a high risk move transporting the beeb from changing table to bath in the buff. But we do it every day. Never had an issue. Then yesterday – backfire….a momentary nude bathside perch yielded an oversized rabbit turd on daddy's leg. And here's how far we've fallen in seven and a half months: didn't faze anybody even for an instant. Just a matter-of-fact kinda 'oh – look-there's a turd on your leg' and an accepting nod……uh, huhhh, yessir there is. I'll bow to the gods of hygiene though and admit this is a laundry worthy event. I'll look the other way if you coat me in barf and/or urine, but these jeans need a washing before I eat off them again.

Posted in Uncategorized

Dammit, would you knock that off?

Posted on November 25, 2012

I really really really really really wish she wouldn't do this with her pile o' rings. I'm cool with the rings themselves…heck, eat each and every one of 'em for all I care. But the yellow bit upon which one is meant to pile said rings? Let's keep that out of our mouth, shall we?

I'm just funnin' with ya, beeb….enjoy your toys and your childhood innocence. I'm only jealous of both.

Posted in pics

The beeb eats the boot

Posted on November 26, 2012

Traveling down to Grandma A's house for Thanksgiving! So ready for the brownest meal of the year that she's wolfing down an appetizer glitter boot. Mmmmmmm.....glitter boot....

Additional pictures forthcoming, but rest assured that we enjoyed some quality family time with both sets of relatives. Lily showed off her standing skills – now able to stand using only one hand for balance! A far cry from walking or even pulling herself up...but clear progress in the areas of strength and coordination...

Many thanks to our host grandparents for opening their home to my band of gypsies. And many thanks to my band of gypsies for making the trek to the host's home. We couldn't have been any happier with the result!

Posted in pics

Teef pending?

Posted on November 28, 2012

Lily must surely be on the verge of teeth…she's cranklepuss all the time, she's eating only begrudgingly, and she'd rather gnaw than suck on a bottle's nipple. We're not accustomed to all the fussiness and truth be told, not diggin' on it too much…but we consider ourselves very lucky if this is all the bad we have to deal with. So fuss on, Miss Fussypants, and let's get these uncomfortable teeth to the outside where they belong. And when they arrive, I shall tell you of the Tooth Fairy and other stalking weirdos that skitter in and out of your room whilst you sleep. Want a fat bearded guy judging you all year? More good news on the way!

Posted in Uncategorized

Back to the basics: reading

Posted on November 29, 2012

Full disclosure: we are not good parents. As evidence….the beeb has been turning against me at bedtime. I mean, she's cool and stuff and she's not swinging on me (intentionally). But she's got no interest in the old man putting her to bed. For a few days there, she would flat refuse – planking and crying and generally being a pain in the neck until mom came in and did the honors. For dad we have…a glass of rejection.

Then last night in a moment of clarity I decided to try the unthinkable…I read to her. And she dug it. She didn't go to sleep, but she was calmed and interested and didn't fight when I plopped her in the bed. She just laid there for a bit and went to sleep. Rapture! I tried it again tonight and it worked like magic. We may be on to something here…

Who knew that reading might be good for a child?! What a notion. I kid somewhat – we have read to her and we thoughtfully encourage her to eat her ABC123 book regularly. But we haven't done bedtime stories for a while. Oooops. No worries – they're back on the menu again and tomorrow I'm going for 3 in a row. Unless, of course, the zookeeper wises up to that wily gorilla and doesn't let him steal the zoo keys. Then we'd have nothing to read about.

Posted in Uncategorized

Lies and the hexapus

Posted on November 30, 2012

OK, so we trust our daughter's education to the providers of educational toys. Who wouldn't, right? You need to – it's the way the system works these days. But then I stumble upon this thing and it rips the whole contract apart. Just what do you see here?

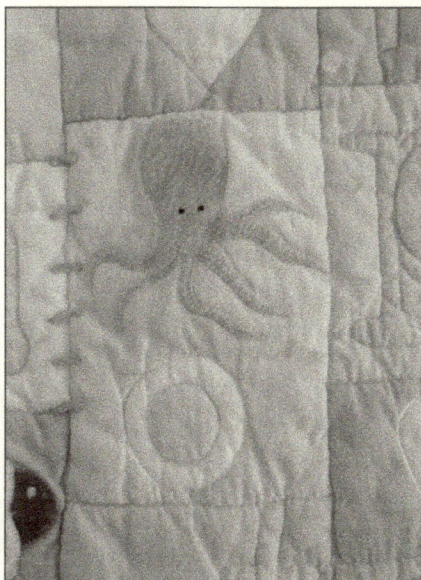

An Octopus, right? And it's on the portion of the patchwork blankey that shows the letter "O". O for Octopus. Easy and done. Well learned, bebus. We're on the right track. But look closer and what do you really see?…

Go ahead – count the tentacles. Six.

It's a goddamn Hexapus, right there on the blanket and filed under "O". What kind of a cruel bastard has the time and evil genius to perpetrate such an injustice?! Warping my bebus…that ain't cool. I'm giving you just two choices, deceitful swine:

Either file it under "H" and allow us to continue our teachings of marine biology and Latin prefixes….

Or sew two more tentacles on that thing so it's accurate.

I'll accept nothing less, and I expect full compliance in short order. There'll be no misleading Hexapus in this household.

Posted in pics | 1 Reply

Hey – lay off the little guy or I'll destroy your entire world. Capisce?

- The Kraken

December

Stuck at work, no bath time tonight

Posted on December 3, 2012

Such a colossal bummer. I got home in time to find mom making dinner, the beeb having already fallen asleep. It was doubly disappointing onnacounta she has evidently grown fond of the Christmas tree and was acting quite overwhelmed by it. I got to hear some of her delightful squeals on the phone. This is a big improvement from yesterday, when she was affirmatively unimpressed by the tree. Man, if only she knew the whole Santa story...that'd blow her little mind. We'll save it for next year and I'll tell her all about it.

Posted in Uncategorized

Acute separation anxiety sucks

Posted on December 4, 2012

It's a bad sign when the nanny asks you, "What did you do to this child?!" on a Monday afternoon. Things got no better on Tuesday either. The issue? Lily doesn't want to be put down and left alone any more. She wants your attention. She wants to be held. She wants to be fussed with and generally noticed. Man, could this be bad news! Or it could be yet another short-lived phase that will leave us scratching our heads in a month or so when she's changed her little mind and moved on to the next thing. I'm hoping that's how it plays out. Today's possible rock bottom: Natalie and Lily were sitting on the floor together. Natalie got up to grab her phone off the table no more than 5 feet away. Lily threw a fit. Crocodile tears (which she's mastered) and the whole bit. Very lame. Better be a phase, beeb…

Posted in Uncategorized

I will eat your toes

Posted on December 5, 2012

Here she is, dressed as the Joker, about to liberate This little piggy (which had plans to go to market) from it's homefoot. Good news, Mom: still no teeth. It had to feel ultraweird to have your toe chomped by the beeb though. Gross.

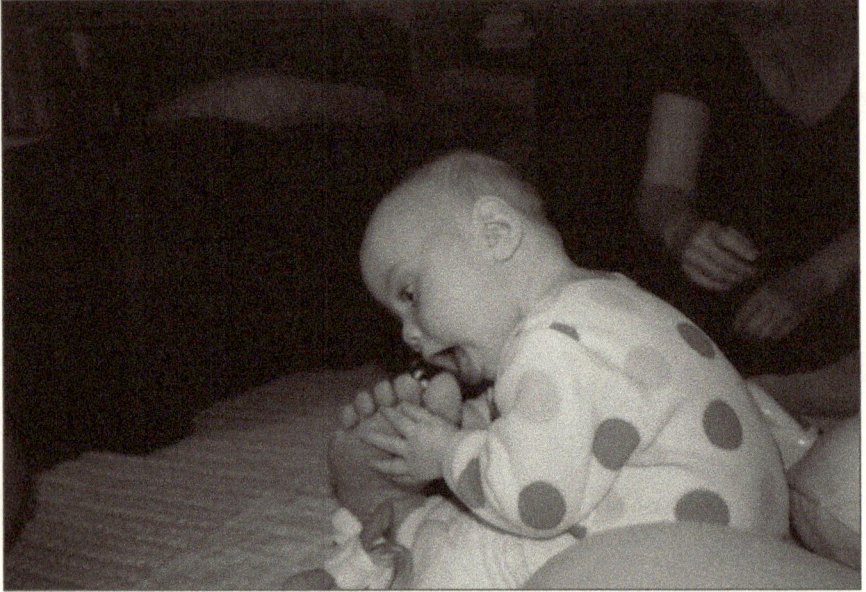

Posted in pics

Parenting definition

Posted on December 6, 2012

Kneebender (noun): a defecation or defecation/urination combination so foul that it causes the party tasked with changing a diaper to wobble and bend at the knees. "Today just before bathtime, Lily delivered a total kneebender." Synonyms: Tearjerker, Cruel bomb, Soul destroyer, Stoolpocalypse. Antonyms: Frous-pous, Air freshener.

My standard apology for toilet humor applies. She friggin' whomped me though.

Posted in Uncategorized

Moonwalking

Posted on December 7, 2012

Our favorite new game Standy-uppy is developing a little bit…the beeb seems to understand that she needs to move her feet in order to matriculate herself down the field. She can't get the forward/backward thing sorted out though. She's moonwalking. It's fantastic. The only down side is that I've got 'Billy Jean' stuck in my head now. I may be purchasing Thriller in the coming days just to purge it.

Posted in Uncategorized

Sick-o.

Posted on December 8, 2012

Well, stupid Dad got everybody sick this weekend. Poor bebus didn't sleep well and we were forced to traumatize her repeatedly with the snot sucker & preliminary saline spray in the nostrils. She does NOT like that. She doesn't even like it when you wipe the snot off her little lip. That confuses me.

Anyway, Mom thought it would cheer her up if she was allowed to wear a tutu and douse herself in pink. The result can be seen below. It's money.

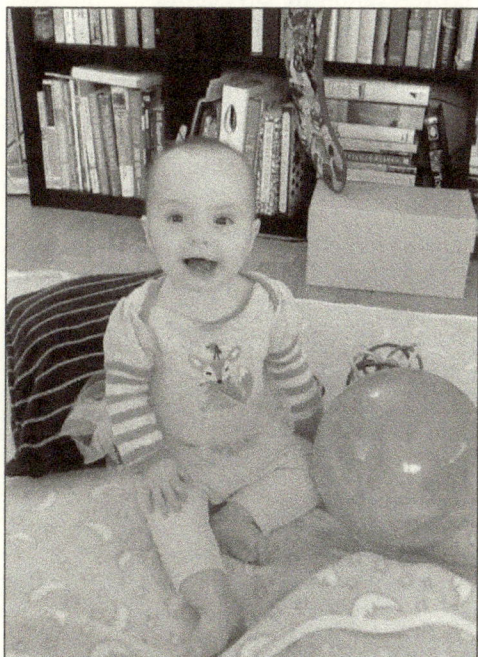

Sorry to report it didn't really distract her from the sneezing, the coughing, the snotting, and the general unhappiness. A quick note on the sneezing: she thinks it's pretty funny. She'll sneeze, normally sneeze again, and then get a big smile on her face like it was a good joke. At least that part's not bothering her.

Posted in pics

Red letter day

Posted on December 9, 2012

It's late so I've got to keep this short, but here's what happened today:

1) We got a somewhat garbled "ma mar" from the beeb (no witnesses, but mom swears it's true).

2) We got a proper "da da" from same. Word up. I'm giving mom the win by a nose but feelin' pretty good about the pronunciation of my admittedly simpler moniker. We both saw it. No foolin!

3) Natalie brokered a meeting with the man in red, Santa himself. Good for a photo of her rummaging through his gin-soaked beard. That pic forthcoming. It's not bad…she even appears happy (ambivalent at a minimum).

Heady days are these as we come down the home stretch in 2012! "Da da." Damn straight!

Posted in Uncategorized | 1 Reply

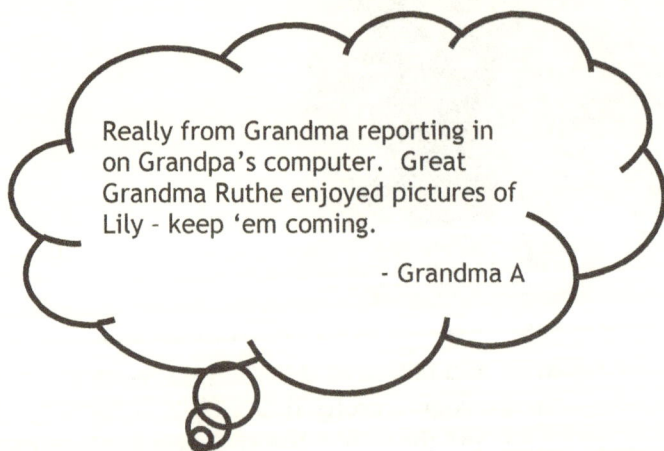

Really from Grandma reporting in on Grandpa's computer. Great Grandma Ruthe enjoyed pictures of Lily - keep 'em coming.

- Grandma A

Lily loves her some Lily

Posted on December 10, 2012

Here's the beeb playing with one of her favorite toys…the mirror. It dates back to the very beginning – we hung it in her crib to keep her calm. The gift that keeps on giving. I present a montage of her staring at herself, including a quick game of the old staple "In your grill"…

Narcissus in da house.

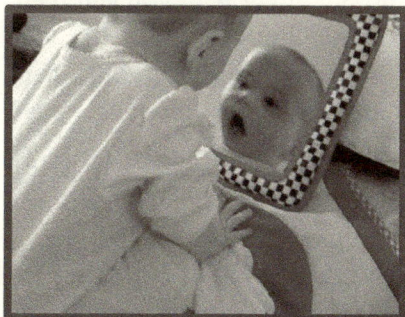

Posted in pics

224

I got punked

Posted on December 11, 2012

Not sure I can prove it, but I swear she was messing with me tonight. She does this thing, see, when she's eating from the bottle. If you put it in her mouth and she didn't invite you to do it, she'll grab it and shove it out of her mouth. So instead, you have to hold it out in front of her, and she'll either 1) open her mouth wide so you can stick it in there, or 2) grab it and direct it toward her mouth. Then she may hold it and she may let go but either way you can feed her for a bit. If she holds it, by the way, sometimes she twists it slowly. That's a trick the nurses in the hospital taught us to keep her sucking – you twist the bottle. Maybe she's trying to convince herself to eat more.

Anyway, we're doing this whole routine tonight just before bedtime. I'm sitting in the recliner, the beeb's sitting on my lap. She's not eating much, so I keep holding out the bottle in front of her. Eventually, she takes it….and then she starts punking me…. She brings it up so that her mouth is not on the nipple but rather just below it on the bottle itself. That ain't gonna work, so I pull the bottle away from her and hold it out again. She grabs it and directs it to herself again – but again her mouth is not on the nipple but on the bottle. The third time, she turns the whole thing entirely upside down and puts her mouth on the bottom of the bottle. And we play this game for a while until she starts (and I swear I am not making this up) putting her mouth in the wrong place *and it's making her laugh and she's sneaking a peek at me watching her!* Sucker Dad doesn't understand that she knows darn well she's doing it wrong and like an idiot I 'help' her, and then she does it wrong again just to watch me react again! Ooooooh, clever and evil bebus! Playing me like a fool.

I'm sure this won't be the last of it, but tonight's the first night I've seen her doing this. You're a quick study, daughter of mine. And I'm thrilled to see the beginnings of a sense of humor, even if I have to be the butt of the joke!

Posted in Uncategorized

American Gothic

Posted on December 12, 2012

Here we are long ago, bored. Not sure why, but the picture don't lie. From June 9th – her 2 month birthday come to think of it. She's 4 times older now. Weird.

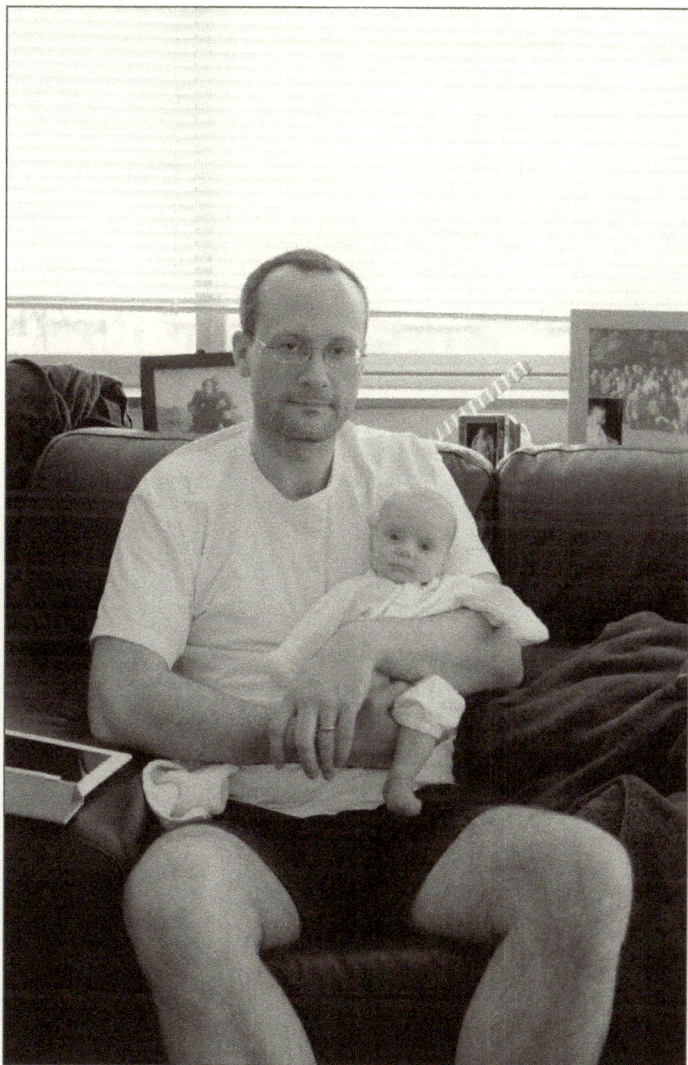

Seriously – moonwalking

Posted on December 13, 2012

Ha! You thought I was making the whole thing up, didn't you?! Well, read 'em and weep…here she is, moonwalking. By that, of course, I mean that she's taking a few tentative steps backwards with plenty of help in her stability. She doesn't have the chops to hang with the King of Pop. Not by a long shot. Hilarious to watch her try to move though. Make sure you've got "Billy Jean" playing (at least in your mind) as you watch…

If you watch very closely, mom makes a brief cameo as well!

Da-da

Posted on December 14, 2012

This video has everything. A great score, a couple of family-renowned actresses, some slapstick, and most importantly some brilliant dialogue. The big payoff comes right at the very end, when Lily chucks out a pure and unadulterated "Da-da" for all the world to see. Superawesome if you happen to be Da-da. And I do. Oh, she flirts with it at first. But it's there, baby.

Full disclosure: it's a loooooong video, aimed at an audience with grandma-level patience. Don't attempt to watch in a single setting unless you really dig bebii.

Posted in Videos | 1 Reply

If anything, too short. Also, awesome flexible MOM and great looking picture wall. (The length of the video allowed some attention to background features.)

- Grandma A

Auntie G in the house

Posted on December 15, 2012

What would YOU do if Auntie G showed up to watch the Steeler's game and they were getting blown out by the pathetic Chargers?! You'd head-butt that bizwatch, that's what. Luckily, the beeb's soft skull prevents her from doing any lasting damage....but she was trying to break some noses (or eat them...or....I don't know...something....).

Gina is just along for the ride. The beeb? In full control of the situation.

(some time passes)

WHOA! I just watched it again and my worst fears are realized. Lily's some kinda demon and she's trying to eat Gina's soul. Check out the sheen in the bebe's eyes just before mom innocently says, "Why is this light on?" Mom: don't you know?! The camera is equipped with proprietary Demon Identification*, which was only offered on that model the very year we bought it!! It explains a lot, really. I'm hoping that admitting her, ahem, situation is the first step toward true healing. I'm also hoping I can stop snipping her little tail off every couple weeks. That damn thing grows back quickly.

*Trademarked

Posted in Meet the bebe, Videos | 1 Reply

Alternate interpretation: she's doing the baby Vulcan Mind Meld or using an alternate body part to plant a kiss on her Auntie G.

- Grandma A

229

Birthday party heist?

Posted on December 16, 2012

We had a grand old time at Miss Teagan's birthday party today! All the necessary ingredients were there: a pile o' kids, a number of balloons, music, even pizza and cake. Lily's not much for restaurant food and we didn't bring our blender…so…she had to settle for a bottle while the other kiddies enjoyed the good stuff. Didn't dampen her spirits in the slightest way. I think she may have gotten into it a little with one of the others – toward the end of our stay, she jumped into what I believe was a '55 Bel Air and fishtailed across the room in a smoky escape attempt. Mom was nimble and grabbed her before she could make it out the door. I was there in time to snap a quick photo.

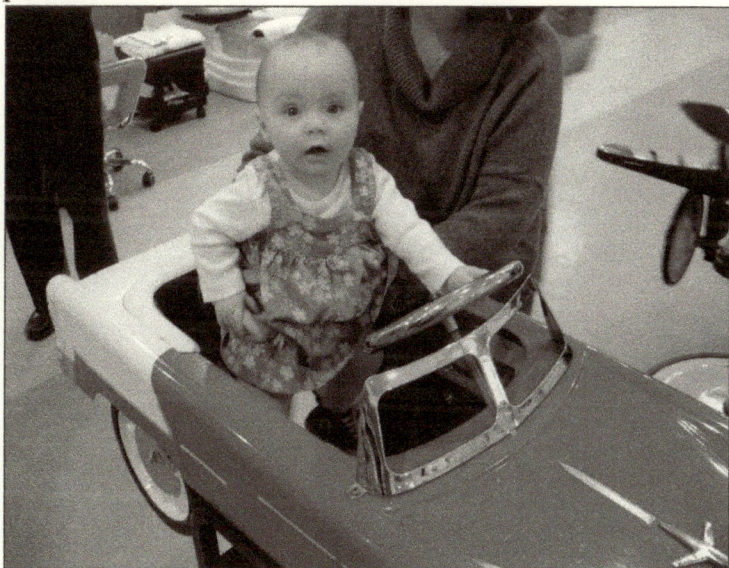

I appreciate the automotive enthusiasm, beeb, but let's get you walking before you drive on public roads, OK? And whatever you said to the other girl, I hope you apologized after we thwarted your plans. Unless she was in on it, too?…hmmmm…I wonder if someone else slipped out the back door with cake while you had us distracted? Clever girl…

Posted in pics

Arboreal delight

Posted on December 17, 2012

Here's young bebus diggin' on the Exmas tree. Sorry – you may prefer the term Crimmas tree. Either is OK with me. In any event, despite the blurry action shot here, you can get a sense of the wonderment and fascination Lily exhibits toward the ol' tree. She was really cautious at first but now enjoys a handful of pine needles and whichever bauble or bangle is closest. Today we augmented with candy canes, which I would love to let her eat…but I'm afraid the potential for disaster is just too great. We could probably avoid the choking hazard, but the damn things turn into glue sticks with a bit of saliva….I don't want her first haircut to be a candycane-ectomy.

Posted in pics

Ready to go, chief

Posted on December 18, 2012

Who looks more prepared for travel than this one? Well done, beeb.

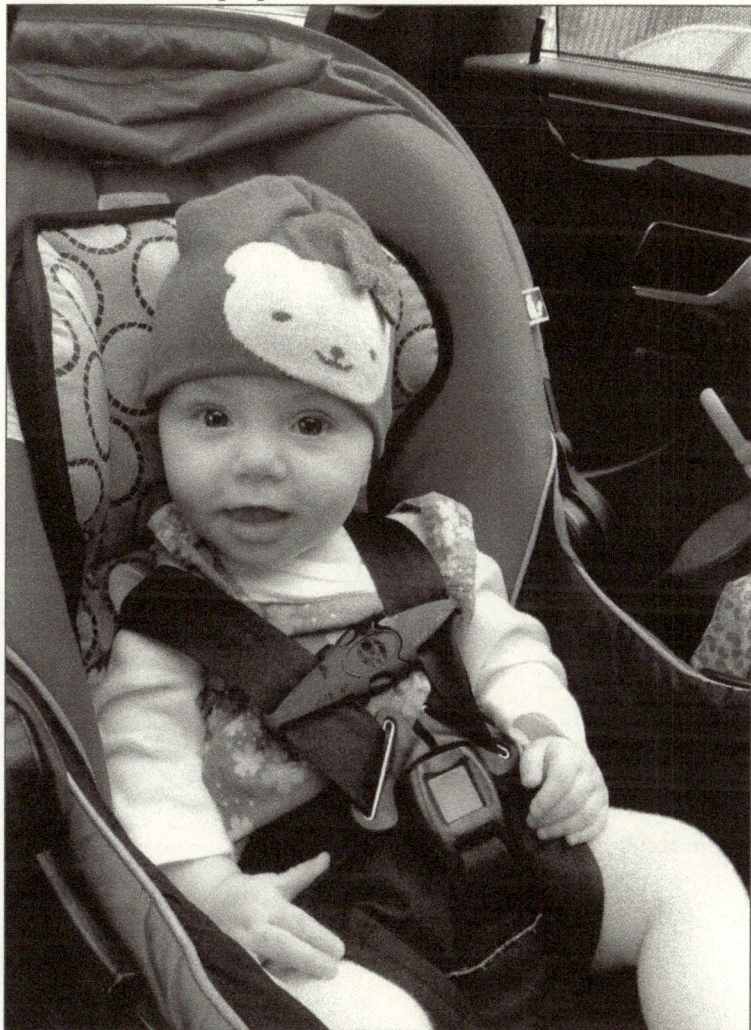

You can't really tell from the photo, but those shoulder straps are permasoaked with spit. Eeeeeeew. Only cute from a distance.

Posted in pics

The Hexapus conspiracy

Posted on December 19, 2012

Ok, so here we go again. New bath toys arrived today. Guess what we got on our hands for the second time?! A freakin' hexapus. Go ahead, count 'em up!

He's a cute little guy, too.

A real shame. Who's denying these mollusks their limbs? Are they on a plan for a 25% reduction in their arms budget?* Did the additional tentacles tear off when they could no longer hold on to the edge of the fiscal cliff?* I don't know what the heck is going on around here, but I am UN-happy with a couple things and the number 8 (which by the way is considered a lucky number by a great number of smart and reputable people) would no doubt agree. The 6 cartel must be stopped.

You know what? I'm going to go and double-check our current bath-time representative to see where he stands…is there already a traitor in our midst?…gimme a minute…..

(Whew) Thank you, symbol of truth and fairness! I knew there was a reason the beeb liked you, old friend. I dub thee "Chad". I nickname thee "Ocho Pusso". And I dig thee.

I guess tomorrow we start explaining numbers and fractions and genetics and all manner of advanced topics. We can't expect young bebus to figure this stuff out on her own.

*Sincere apologies. Really bad joke.

Boring day

Posted on December 21, 2012

Nothing new or noteworthy today. Heard a rumor of teeth making an appearance on the south gum, but cursory investigation revealed nothing. Yep, just another day in beebdom over here...she doesn't want to nap, got pissy when we tried to put her to sleep, and tried to eat her new bathtoy's eyes. I did my fatherly duties, shouting "Eat 'em, girl! Eat 'em in the eyes!!" Don't know if she recognizes how important that sort of encouragement is during the formative years. Decades from now, when she is successfully eating people in their eyes, I hope she can look back on this and smile. I know I will.

Posted in Uncategorized

Observation: she grabs with a purpose

Posted on December 22, 2012

Miss Lily has taken to grabbing daddy's face a little more often, and let me tell you she doesn't go lightly. Today, she reached out and grabbed my nose. In the course of doing so, she got her thumb up my left nostril and dug it into a portion of my brain that's hard wired for pain. And she grabbed. I mean, she GRABBED my nose with her thumb in my pain brain and she smiled ever so sweetly at me. It's cute, but cute like being covered in adorable puppies who are nipping at you with their needle sharp teeth. I suppose it serves a purpose – she must be learning something. Let me believe that anyway…I don't want to think that was in vain.

Posted in Uncategorized

Lily on piano, mom on finance

Posted on December 23, 2012

Well, this is fairly typical I gotta say. The beeb's having a blast banging away at the piano. Dad is enamored as he so often is. Mom? Mom's in her own world, and if you listen closely you'll hear she's discussing mutual funds and the correct allocation of assets between them. Luckily for us, she doesn't realize there's a camera running. Priceless!

Oooooh – double bonus! I didn't realize until I listened to it again…mom dresses me down for recording it. Fantastic.

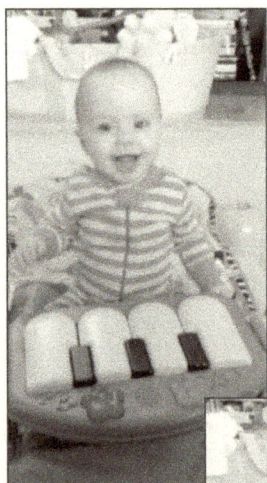

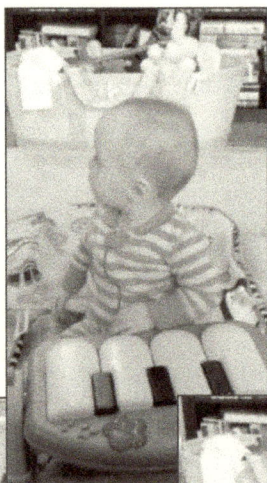

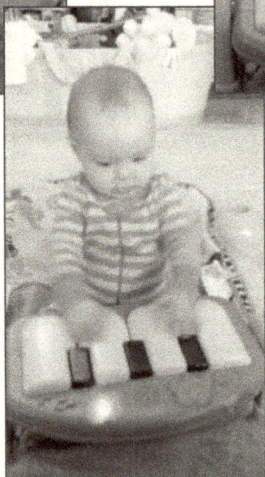

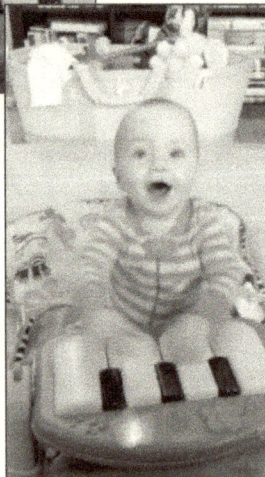

First vegetable tooth

Posted on December 24, 2012

Here's the beeb at lunch today. Noteworthy:
1. First tooth! It's orange and made of carrot mush but what the heck. Others will follow shortly I'm sure. (can you see it in there?!)
2. How 'bout that insurance salesman pose? Arm cocked and resting casually on the table...hey, trust me, ok?...you can't lose!...
3. Pink cheeks = teef on the way? Visiting dignitaries told us yesterday that flushed cheeks were a sure sign of teething. Could be 'Go' time on the ivories.

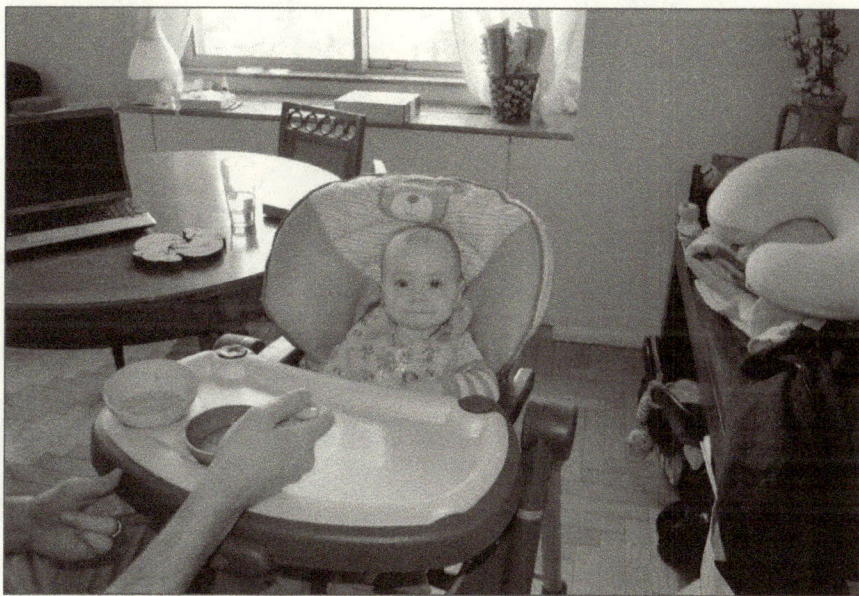

Grandma and grandpa were there to heckle and take photos. This one displays an excellent ancillary view of me flipping off nobody in particular.

Posted in pics

Greetings from Sedona

Posted on December 25, 2012

This one from Gma and Gpa on the daddy side…a vintage look at Sedona in September. She's looking super-double-coy and damn near adorable if you ask me. This was right before mom found a mousetrap in the shower and then hopped with broken toes to the bed, only to sit on a whoopie cushion. That angelic face is hiding something… Had I time to photoshop it, I'd draw on her little horns.

Posted in Flashback, pics

Xmas hippo

Posted on December 26, 2012

Oh boy, oh boy! It took a little while to get her going, but the beeb dug on the Crimmas thing and despite being a rookie…she unwrapped, she freaked out, and she generally behaved like a veteran. I would give my pinkie toe to have (ahem) footage of her opening her cool hippo. Sadly, it is not to be. What we do have is some video of the time shortly thereafter. I think she's s'plaining things to the idiot adults in the room (my wife, myself, and my parents). We clearly don't get it. But the bebe does!

Lily with the hippo

There's a medium paparazzi presence if you watch closely.

Posted in pics | 1 Reply

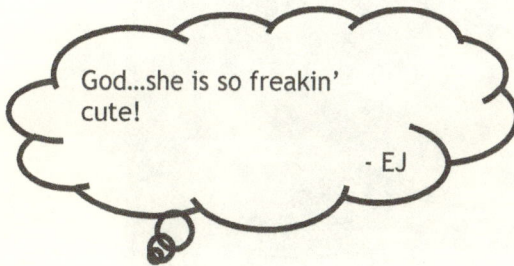

God...she is so freakin' cute!

- EJ

Exersaucer in the Evening

Posted on December 27, 2012

I am honored and overwhelmed to be guest blogging, but the real fun is being the guest nanny for a few days. I am under strict orders from the real nanny not to ``break`` her. I am doing my best, but it's a challenge not to spoil her. This is Miss Lily in her exersaucer, having a blast and bouncing to beat the band.

- Grandma A

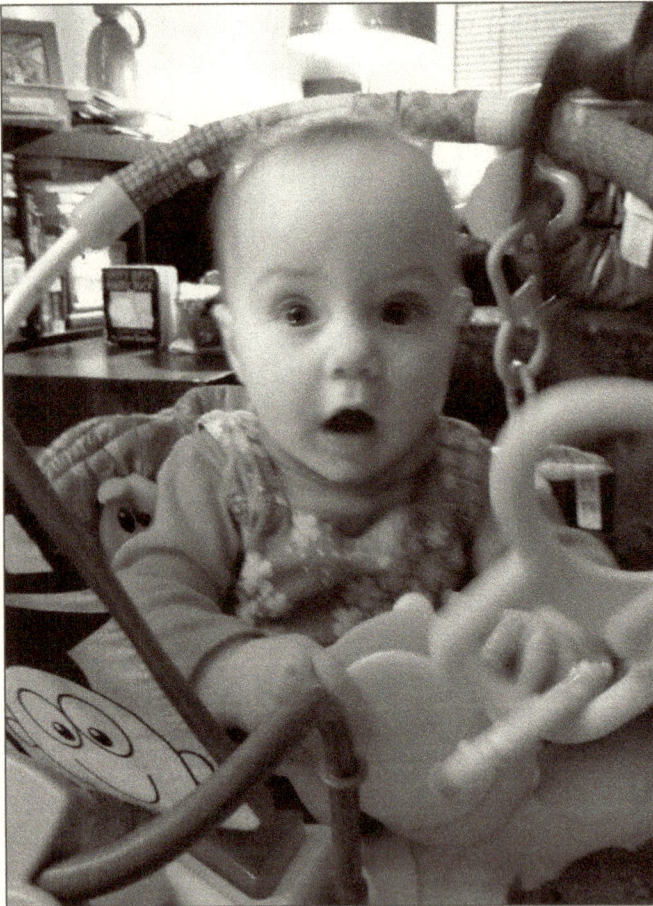

Posted in Guest Post!, pics

Yeaaaahhhhhh!

Posted on December 28, 2012

Oh, so the beeb is getting expressive now! She's learned a combo grunt/yell that sounds like Yeaaaahhhhhh!…and she's throwing it around quite liberally. It's normally accompanied by a wide open face (particularly the eyes and mouth, but I'd swear her little ears and nose are somehow flaring as well). It's a total scene. Here's how it normally goes: Lily is playing with something (anything), and either pulls it to her chest or else lets go and clasps her hands, opens her face, and goes: "Yeaaaahhhhhh!" It's clear she's trying to elicit a response and this morning Mama, Grandma A, and I participated in an extended back-and-forth. We could have been watching a game that was going well for our team, if you just looked at the dialog.

This appears to be unrelated to teething, but good Lord is she teething. We can still see bumps in her bottom gum showing where the teeth are working their way up, but they're awfully shy and not yet willing to make a formal appearance. The beeb is on-and-off grumpy, presumably due to mouth pains. She's not eating as readily lately and she wants to chew on everything including her own hand. How much of her hand fits in her mouth, you ask? All of it. I've seen it. It's not pretty. It's a slobberfest nobody asked for.

Also a slobberfest: the slinky. She looooves that slinky, but it has much more surface area than I ever considered. Surface area is a good proxy for amount of drool something can hold….and this something is a spring-loaded weapon of mass salivation. Think squirt gun + oscillating fan. Now think laundry requirements. Welcome to my life.

Posted in Uncategorized

Two generations doting on one

Posted on December 30, 2012

A quick pic from the tail end of the visit by Gma A. Not hard to see that mom and grandma are obsessed with the beeb, and the beeb is obsessed with the camera. I was just trying to take a photo of the Christmas tree (with which I was obsessed) and these three knobs got in the way….

Posted in Meet the bebe, pics

243

Rockin the 80's look

Posted on December 31, 2012

Lily dressed for any rock concert from around 1981 to around 1988. The jeans aren't acid washed, but they're looking sharp. I think she's got a switchblade in her back pocket....and she might use it to separate you from your Air Jordans.

I told her she had to be back by midnight, and she was all like, "Oh yeah?! And what if I'm not, old man? I don't have to listen to you!" Then everything went slow motion and I heard Alice Cooper's 'No More Mr. Nice Guy' playing from nowhere in particular as the beeb walked out to her Z28. It was a strange scene.

Posted in Uncategorized

www.ingramcontent.com/pod-product-compliance
Lightning Source LLC
Chambersburg PA
CBHW021050090426
42738CB00006B/263